The Keto Diet

**The Complete Guide To The Ketogenic Diet For Beginners
Delicious, Simple and Easy Keto Recipes To Heal Your Body,
Shed Weight and Regain Your Confidence**

Table of Contents

Introduction

The ketogenic diet, sometimes referred to as a "keto" diet for short, is a way of eating that takes advantage of your body's metabolic tendencies to produce weight loss and other beneficial biological reactions. A keto diet primarily revolves around a significantly reduced intake of carbohydrates, usually with a corresponding increase in the intake of fats and proteins, so it's sometimes also referred to as a "low carb" or a "low carb/high fat" diet.

It's the reduction in carbs that packs the keto diet's real punch, though, and that's the focus of most keto recipes. Keto recipes eliminate the sources of carbohydrates that make up the bulk of traditional Western diets—grains, breads, pasta, starches, and sugars—and emphasize instead meats and other proteins, as well as relatively low-carb vegetables and fruits.

The Ketogenic Diet

The ketogenic diet was originally developed as a therapy to improve neurological function in epileptics, but its wide-ranging metabolic and nutritional benefits have led millions to pursue keto programs as part of their complete nutritional plans. While weight loss is not the only benefit of a keto diet, many weight-loss programs are designed to produce a ketogenic phase that helps to shift the body's metabolism into a state more conducive to burning stored fat.

What is the Ketogenic Diet?

In the strictest sense, a ketogenic diet is a nutritional program that focuses on relatively high fat intake, moderate protein intake, and low carbohydrate intake. The goal of the diet is to force the body to burn fat as fuel rather than carbohydrates, the fuel that the metabolic system leans on most heavily under normal conditions. The hope is that the body will become conditioned to burning fat stores--and thereby kick starting weight loss--rather than relying on carbohydrate fuels and simply storing fat.

The Beginning of Ketosis

Typically, the human body produces energy by converting carbohydrates in food into glucose and then burning that glucose in its cells. Carbohydrates are relatively easy for the body to convert into glucose, making them an ideal fuel source, and the body's metabolic system will rely on them when it can, fueling itself with carbohydrates as they enter the digestive system from food and leaving stored fat in place.

When excess carbohydrates are consumed, the metabolic system converts any carbs it doesn't need for fuel into fat and stores that fat in the body. Then the body resists burning that stored fat, opting instead to burn freshly consumed carbs, and the cycle starts over again.

However, if sufficient carbohydrates aren't present in a person's diet, the body will be forced to look elsewhere for the energy it needs. The next most preferred fuel source is fat, which is metabolized in the liver. The liver turns fat into fatty acids and other water-soluble molecules called ketone bodies, which can be used in the body's cells as a fuel source. When the liver is actively metabolizing fat and the level of ketone bodies in the blood stream is elevated above typical levels, the body is said to have entered a state of ketosis.

Harnessing Ketosis

The ketogenic diet was originally developed as a therapeutic diet for patients with epilepsy. Research indicated that when patients' brain activity was fueled by ketone bodies instead of by glucose, the frequency of epileptic seizures in study subjects decreased. The therapeutic diet was first developed in the 1920s and although it gradually fell out of favor because of the advent of pharmaceutical therapies for epilepsy, the diet experienced a revival in interest among clinicians in the 1990s. That's when some dietary researchers began to incorporate elements of a ketogenic diet into their low-carbohydrate regimens even for those who were not struggling with epilepsy.

The popular low-carb diets of the 1990s and early 2000s attempted to harness ketosis by guiding adherents through an initial phase during which carbohydrate intake was drastically reduced. The theory was that by producing ketosis through severely limited carb intake, the body would shift to a fat-burning mode, triggering an initial rapid weight loss that could be sustained even when carbohydrate intake was moderately increased later in the program. These approaches also emphasized diets that would inhibit the production of insulin, which aids in the processing of glucose and inhibits the metabolic processing of fats.

What are the Benefits of a Ketogenic Diet?

Weight loss

The promise of rapid, dramatic weight loss is the lure of the keto diet for many of adherents. It's not uncommon for a keto diet to produce weight loss of several pounds in the first week or so, and it's hard to resist the possibility to such a quick result. Everyone who tries a keto diet will experience something different, however, and consistent, sustained weight loss will only happen when you dedicate careful attention to your food intake and exercise program.

The big initial weight loss that often accompanies the beginning of keto diet is generally attributable to a loss of your body's water content. As you shift the proportion of nutrients you take in, your body will attempt to adjust to the new order of things, and part of that adjustment is typically the release of a significant amount of water. Fluid loss can account for the loss of up to 10 pounds of weight in the first week of a diet.

This initial weight loss is only the beginning, though. The water loss is an indication that your body is changing the way it processes nutrients, and it's the first step in moving your metabolism toward a state of ketosis. As you continue to follow the diet, your weight loss is likely to slow, but the weight loss is theoretically more like to come from the metabolism of stored fat, which is the overall goal of the diet program.

Blood Sugar Control

Remember how we said that your body can easily convert carbohydrates into fuel? That means that when you eat lots of carbs, your body can very easily turn those carbs into the glucose that your cells can use as fuel. The glucose is transported through your blood stream, so high carbohydrate intake can result in significant spikes in your blood sugar (glucose) level.

A keto diet can help to eliminate spikes in blood sugar levels by giving your body fats and proteins to process instead of carbs. These nutrients are not as readily converted to glucose, so blood sugar spikes are not nearly as likely to occur when you eat more of them and fewer carbs.

Appetite Control

The flip side to a blood sugar spike is a blood sugar crash that comes after your cells quickly devour the glucose produced by high carbohydrate consumption. Carbs are processed and consumed quickly, leaving your body wanting more after they're all gone. It's a roller coaster ride for your body in terms of energy, and it plays havoc with your appetite. Eat a bunch of carbs and you might feel full in the moment, but you're likely to be hungry again in a ridiculously short time.

A keto diet can help to stabilize your appetite and eliminate cravings by reducing the ups and downs caused by high carb intake. A diet high in fats and proteins can help you to feel full faster and stave off hunger longer than a diet that relies too heavily on carbohydrates.

Energy Levels

Another benefit of stabilized blood sugar is the stabilization of your energy level throughout the day. When your blood sugar level crashes, you not only get hungry, you also get tired. Without carbs to provide quick and easy energy, your body doesn't think it has anywhere to turn, so it simply gives up and gets lethargic until it convinces you to eat more carbs.

Your body on a keto diet behaves differently. After you've trained your body to enter a state of ketosis, it knows where to look for energy when there are no carbs readily available. There's plenty of energy to be found in your stored fat, and a body that's used to a keto diet is able to utilize that energy to keep you from feeling tired and lethargic even between meals.

Keto Diet and Insulin Resistance

Insulin is a hormone that allows your body to process glucose. Your body's production of insulin is a natural process that is crucial to controlling the level of glucose in your blood and fueling your cells. Some people, however, develop insulin resistance, which means that insulin becomes less effective at processing glucose in their bodies, leading to elevated blood sugar levels and potentially serious health problems.

A keto diet helps to sidestep the problems of insulin resistance by stabilizing blood sugar levels. Your body becomes less dependent on insulin production, and the impact of insulin resistance is decreased, too.

What are Carbohydrates, Fats and Proteins?

Now you know how a keto diet works to help your body to process fats, proteins and carbohydrates, but to fully understand the benefits of keto, you need to understand what fats, proteins and carbs are in the first place.

Fats, proteins, and carbohydrates are compounds called macronutrients. They are categories of substances that fuel our metabolic processes, and we need large amounts of them in order to live. In various combinations, these three types of macronutrients make up most of the foods we eat.

Carbohydrates (or "carbs" for short) make up the bulk of the foods in the typical Western diet. They are chemical compounds that contain carbon, hydrogen, and oxygen, and as we have already learned, they're easily processed by the body into cell-fueling glucose. Common carbohydrates include the fructose sugar in fruits, the lactose sugar in dairy products, and the sucrose in common table sugar. The starches and cellulose in vegetables are also carbohydrates.

Proteins are compounds made up of chains of amino acids. They are not as easily used by the body for fuel, but they are vital for other cell functions, maintenance, and repair. In our diet, proteins primarily come from animal products such as meat or eggs, but they can also be found in some plant-based foods such as nuts and legumes.

Fats are compounds consisting of chains of fatty acids. As a nutrient, fats are an excellent source of energy, but under typical metabolic conditions, they're more often used as a way to store energy for later use. Fatty acids are stored in specialized tissues in the body, and they're only used for energy when necessary. In the diet, fats can come from either animal or plant sources.

How is a Ketogenic Diet Structured?

Remember that the goal of a keto diet is to force your body into a state of ketosis. That's when your body has begun metabolizing fat in your liver and producing ketone bodies to help fuel your cells. Your body will only enter a state of ketosis when it has to; as long as it has an adequate supply of easy-to-use carbohydrates at its disposal, it will continue burning them. When it runs out of carbs, it will simply demand more by making you hungry. It will not, however, work very hard to burn stored fat.

If, however, you convince your body that no more carbs are on the way, it will have no choice but to resort to ketosis and start burning fat. The only way that's going to happen is if you severely limit your intake of carbohydrates and correspondingly increase your intake of the other two macronutrients.

The ideal ratio of macronutrients for a keto diet will vary from person to person depending on factors such as age, weight, body fat percentage, and activity level. However, some general goals can help you to structure your diet to give you the best chance of pushing your body into a state of ketosis.

First of all, and most importantly, your diet must include a very low proportion of carbohydrates. In most cases, carbohydrates shouldn't make up more than five percent of the macronutrients you consume, and even lower levels of carb consumption are sometimes necessary. This is virtually the opposite of the mainstream Western diet and often the hardest part of the keto diet to pull off.

Keto diets usually include a moderate intake of proteins, generally somewhere between 15 and 35 percent of all the macronutrients you take in. It's important to maintain moderate protein consumption, because low protein intake can lead to situations that undermine the benefits of the keto diet.

Fats typically make up the majority of macronutrients in a keto diet, with the proportion usually falling between 60 and 80 percent. The goal is to transform fats into your body's primary fuel source, so you need lots of them.

With each recipe in this book, we've included an estimate of the amount of carbohydrates, fats, and protein in the finished dishes. These numbers are estimates only—the actual nutrient content of the dishes will vary depending on the specifics of the ingredients and how they're prepared—but you can use them as a starting point for planning your diet.

The Best Keto Foods

When you're on a keto diet, foods high in fats and protein are your friend, although you should look for the healthiest versions of these foods. You can safely eat meats, fish, poultry, and eggs. There are also plenty of plant-based fats that fit well into a keto diet, including olive oil, coconut oil, and avocado. You can also feel good about eating most leafy vegetables and greens.

Other foods that contain a balance of carbohydrates, fats and proteins should be eaten less often but can still be part of a keto diet. These foods include dairy products, nuts, root vegetables, cabbage, cauliflower, broccoli, tomatoes, peppers, and mushrooms.

Foods to Avoid

To make a keto diet successful, you have to steer clear of foods that are high in carbohydrates. That means you need to avoid grains and foods made from them (including breads, pasta, and rice), legumes (like beans and peas), starchy vegetables (potatoes, carrots, corn), sugars (including honey and syrups), and most fruits.

This doesn't mean you can never eat any of these foods, but you have to be very aware of their relatively high carbohydrate content. You're best staying away from bread altogether, but occasionally including beans or peas in your dishes can be acceptable.

What are the Dangers of the Ketogenic Diet?

A keto diet has many benefits, but in some rare cases, it can have some side effects. Before you embark on a keto program, you should be aware of its potential pitfalls.

Ketoacidosis

Ketoacidosis is a potentially very serious metabolic condition that results from a combination of high ketone levels and high blood sugar levels in the bloodstream. It is most often a complication of type 1 diabetes, and it is very rare in people without diabetes. However, because the name of the condition is so similar to the state of ketosis encouraged by a keto diet, the two states are often confused. In reality, healthy people should have no reason to be concerned that a keto diet will trigger ketoacidosis.

Keto Flu

As you begin the keto diet, you will be pushing your body to change the way it fuels itself. As you shift from a carbohydrate fuel source to the fat fuel source used during ketosis, you're likely to encounter an interim period during which your body isn't quite sure where it should look for fuel.

During this time before ketosis really kicks in, some people experience lethargy, grogginess, or other minor ill feelings. Sometimes referred to as "keto flu," this unpleasant effect will almost always dissipate in just a few days as your body adjusts to the diet.

Constipation

Constipation is a common problem among people who are new to the keto diet. The problem is likely caused by the loss of fluid triggered by the sudden change in diet, as well as the likelihood that you're eating less fiber in a low-carb diet. The solution is usually to be sure that you're drinking plenty of water and eating leafy vegetables that contain a relatively high amount of fiber.

Low Physical Performance

Athletes are often concerned that a low-carb diet will result in reduced athletic performance since their bodies are trained to use carbohydrates as their main energy source. If your athletic activity requires you to perform at high intensity for a short time, you might experience a degradation in your performance while you're on a keto diet.

While that might be true for athletes who need high energy levels for short bursts of time, endurance athletes know that being able to tap into fat stores for energy can actually increase performance. During endurance sports such as distance running, performance increases when an athlete is able to access energy in stored fat after readily available carbs are gone.

Ask Your Doctor

As is the case with any diet or nutrition program, a keto diet isn't for everyone. While it delivers measurable benefits for most people, the keto diet depends on a dramatic shift away from the typical balance of dietary nutrients, and such a dramatic shift can exacerbate some existing health conditions and may trigger others.

Before you begin a keto diet—or any other diet, for that matter—you should always consult with a doctor or other medical professional to be sure that it's safe for you to alter your food intake in the ways demanded by the keto. You should also pay close attention to how your body is responding to the diet as you progress, and if something doesn't feel right, consult your doctor.

Recipes

Following a ketogenic diet requires you to make some big changes to the way you eat, and that can be a challenge, especially for busy people who don't have the time to learn a whole new way of cooking and meal planning.

The recipes we've included here are full of flavor and variety. They get the most from the limitations of the keto diet, allowing you to have a new keto-friendly dish every day of the week if you want. Best of all, the simplicity of the recipes ensures that anyone, no matter how pressed for time, can fit a keto diet into their lifestyle.

Smoothies and Breakfast

A keto diet has plenty of room in it for classic breakfast foods like eggs and bacon, but your keto breakfast doesn't have to stick to the boring basics. These recipes will give you new twists on old favorites so you can start every day in a keto way.

Red and Green Keto Smoothie

Servings: 2
Time Required: About 5 minutes

Ingredients:
- 1 ripe avocado, peeled and pitted
- 1 1/3 cup water
- 3 Tbsp. lemon juice
- 4 tsp. sugar substitute
- ½ cup frozen unsweetened raspberries

Directions:
1. Add all ingredients to blender.
2. Blend until smooth.
3. Divide into two equal servings in tall glasses.

Nutrition Information Per Serving
- Total Fat: 20 grams
- Carbohydrates: 13 grams
- Protein: 2.5 grams

Pumpkin Smoothie

Servings: 2
Time Required: About 5 minutes

Ingredients:
- ¼ cup pumpkin purée
- ¼ cup water
- ¼ cup vanilla whey protein
- ¼ cup sour cream
- ½ tsp. pumpkin pie spice mix
- 1 tsp. sugar substitute
- 1 Tbsp. coconut oil
- ¼ cup whipped cream

Directions:
1. Place all the ingredients into a blender and pulse until smooth.
2. Divide into two equal servings in tall glasses.

Nutrition Information Per Serving
- Total Fat: 33 grams
- Carbohydrates: 10 grams
- Protein: 22 grams

Peanut Butter Smoothie

Servings: 1
Time Required: About 5 minutes

Ingredients:
- ½ cup unsweetened almond milk
- ½ cup low-fat cottage cheese
- 1 Tbsp. sugar-free natural peanut butter
- 1 cup ice
- 1 tsp. sugar substitute

Directions:
Combine all ingredients in blender and pulse until smooth.

Nutrition Information Per Serving
- Total Fat: 9 grams
- Carbohydrates: 10 grams
- Protein: 18 grams

Slow Cooker Ham and Egg Scramble

Servings: 6
Time Required: About 4.5 hours

Ingredients:
- 1 onion, diced
- 2 cups cooked ham, cubed
- 2 cups cheddar cheese, grated
- 10 eggs
- 1 cup whole milk
- 1 tsp. salt
- 1 tsp. pepper

Directions:
1. Place ham, onion, and cheese in the Instant Pot.
2. In a mixing bowl, whisk together the milk and eggs until the eggs are beaten. Add salt and pepper and stir to mix thoroughly.
3. Poor the egg mixture over the ingredients in a slow cooker.
4. Cover the pot and cook on low for 4 hours.
5. Serve hot.

Nutrition Information Per Serving
- Total Fat: 11 grams
- Carbohydrates: 3 grams
- Protein: 11 grams

Pressure Cooker Soft-Boiled Eggs

Servings: 6
Time Required: About 10 minutes

Ingredients:
- 6 large eggs
- ¾ cup water

Directions:
1. Put the steamer rack into your pressure cooker and pour in the water.
2. Place eggs, still in the shell, on top of the steamer rack.
3. Cover and lock the pot.
4. Using the Steam function, set the cook time to 2 minutes.
5. When the cook time is up, remove the eggs and serve hot.

Nutrition Information Per Serving
- Total Fat: 5 grams
- Carbohydrates: 0 grams
- Protein: 6 grams

Omelets in a Cup

Servings: 4
Time Required: About 20 minutes

Ingredients:
- 4 eggs
- ½ cup onion, diced
- ½ cup bell pepper, diced
- ½ cup cheddar cheese, grated
- ¼ cup half and half

Directions:
1. In a mixing bowl, whisk together all ingredients until the eggs are beaten and everything is well combined. Season with salt and pepper.
2. Divide the mixture between four small canning jars. Loosely screw the lids onto the jars.
3. Place a steamer rack in a double boiler/steamer and pour 2 cups water into the pot.
4. Place the jars on the steamer rack.
5. Cover the pot.
6. Bring water to a boil and steam for 10 minutes.
7. Remove the jars from the pot and serve the eggs in the jars.

Nutrition Information Per Serving
- Total Fat: 9 grams
- Carbohydrates: 2 grams
- Protein: 9 grams

Bacon Cups

Servings: 6
Time Required: About 25 minutes

Ingredients:
- 4 eggs
- ¼ cup egg whites
- 4 slices bacon, cooked crisp and crumbled
- ½ cup reduced-fat cottage cheese
- ¼ cup heavy cream
- 1 bell pepper, diced
- ½ onion, diced
- 1 cup cheddar cheese, grated
- 1 cup water

Directions:
1. Combine eggs and egg whites with cheese, cream and cottage cheese in a food processer or blender. Season with salt and pepper. Blend until the ingredients are well combined and smooth, about 30 seconds to a minute.
2. Place a steamer rack in a double boiler/steamer and pour 2 cups water into the pot.
3. Divide the egg mixture evenly between six small canning jars. Top each jar with equal amounts of pepper, onion and bacon crumbles. Put the lids on each jar, but do not tighten the lids tightly.
4. Cover the pot.
5. Bring the water to a boil and steam for 15 minutes.
6. After a few minutes of cooling, the cooked eggs should slide out of the jars, or you can serve them in the jars.

Nutrition Information Per Serving
- Total Fat: 8 grams
- Carbohydrates: 3 grams
- Protein: 9 grams

Pressure Cooker Keto Yogurt

Servings: 6
Time Required: About 10 hours

Ingredients:
- ½ gallon whole milk
- 2 Tbsp. yogurt with live yogurt cultures

Directions:
1. Pour milk into an electronic pressure cooker with a Yogurt setting.
2. Press the Yogurt button and adjust the mode to the "boil" setting.
3. Stir the milk regularly as it slowly comes to a boil to evenly distribute heat through the liquid.
4. During this process, fill a large container (large enough to hold the pot liner) or sink with ice water.
5. When the pressure cooker indicates that the yogurt boil cycle is finished, check the temperature of the milk with a thermometer. If the milk is not yet at 180 degrees Fahrenheit, run the cycle again.
6. Once the milk is at 180 degrees, carefully remove the pot liner and place it in the ice-water bath. Using the thermometer, keep an eye on the milk's temperature until it reaches 110 degrees.
7. At this point, put the liner back into the pressure cooker.
8. Put the 2 tablespoons of active yogurt in a small bowl and slowly add about 3 tablespoons of the warm milk from the pot. This step tempers the yogurt so that the yogurt cultures survive the transfer to the warm milk.
9. Stir the yogurt into the milk in the pot after it's tempered.
10. Cover and look the pot.
11. Push the Yogurt button and adjust the mode to "normal." Set the cook time to at least 10 hours. The longer the yogurt is processed, the less sweet it will be.
12. After 10 hours, the milk should be transformed into a much thicker yogurt. At this stage, remove the pot liner and place it in the refrigerator for about 4 hours.
13. If you'd like a thicker Greek-style yogurt, line a colander with cheese cloth and place it in a large bowl. Put the yogurt into the colander and allow the liquid whey to drain from the yogurt into the bowl.
14. When the yogurt is at the desired consistency, refrigerate it or serve it immediately.

Nutrition Information Per Serving:

- Total Fat: 4 grams
- Carbohydrates: 8 grams
- Protein: 20 grams

Mini Mushroom Keto Quiche

Servings: 6
Time Required: About 20 minutes

Ingredients:
- ½ cup Swiss cheese, grated
- ¼ cup fresh mushrooms, chopped
- ¼ cup spring onion, diced
- 4 eggs
- ¼ cup milk
- 1 cup water

Directions:
1. Using a silicone or heat-proof egg tray, divide the cheese evenly between the cups in the tray, pressing the cheese into the bottom of the cups.
2. Divide the mushrooms and onions among the cups, placing them on top of the cheese.
3. Combine eggs with in a food processor or blender. Season with salt and pepper. Blend until the ingredients are well combined and smooth, about 30 seconds to a minute. Pour the mixture into the cups on top of the cheese, mushrooms and onions.
4. Place the steamer rack in a steamer pot and add the water.
5. Carefully place the tray on top of the steamer rack.
6. Cover the pot.
7. Bring the water to a boil and steam for 15 minutes.
8. After a few minutes of cooling, pop the mini quiches out of the tray and serve immediately.

Nutrition Information Per Serving:
Total Fat: 8 grams
Carbohydrates: 3 grams
Protein: 9 grams

Appetizers, Snacks and Soups

Many of these recipes are designed with the ultimate convenience in mind, and whenever possible, we've gone with a fix-it-and-forget it approach. With many of these soup and stew recipes, all you'll have to do is dump the ingredients into the pot and start a cooking cycle. In a remarkably short time, you'll have a delicious keto-compliant soup. That doesn't mean, though, that you'll have an *ordinary* soup. We've included a range of recipes that draw on the spices and ingredients of international cuisines to keep your keto menu exciting.

Chili Bacon Crab Dip

Servings: 8-10
Time Required: 30 minutes

Ingredients:
- 12 oz. lump crabmeat
- 8 strips thick-cut bacon
- 8 oz. cream cheese, softened
- ½ cup sour cream
- ½ cup mayonnaise
- 2 poblano peppers, seeded and diced
- 4 green onions, diced
- 4 garlic cloves, minced
- 2 Tbsp. fresh lemon juice
- ½ cup of shaved Parmesan cheese

Directions:
1. Preheat oven to 350 degrees.
2. Heat a medium-sized sauté pan on medium-high, then sauté the bacon until it's crisp.
3. Drain the fat from the pan and transfer the bacon to a paper towel to cool.
4. With an electric mixer, combine cream cheese, sour cream and mayonnaise.
5. Add green onion, poblano, garlic, bacon, lemon juice and Parmesan cheese. Mix on low until just combined.
6. Add crabmeat and fold in with a rubber spatula.

7. Pour mixture into a baking dish. Spread into an even layer.
8. Bake for about 20 minutes, until the dip is slightly browned on top and bubbling.

Nutrition Information Per Serving:
- Total Fat: 22 grams
- Carbohydrates: 2 grams
- Protein: 4 grams

Garlic Bacon Dip

Servings: 8-10
Time Required: 30 minutes

Ingredients:

- 6 slices bacon
- 8 oz. cream cheese, softened
- ½ cup sour cream
- 5 oz. fresh spinach
- 2 ½ oz. Parmesan cheese, grated
- 1 ½ Tbsp. chopped fresh parsley
- 1 Tbsp. minced garlic
- 1 Tbsp. lemon juice
- Salt and pepper to taste

Directions:

1. Allow cream cheese to soften at room temperature.
2. Heat a medium-sized sauté pan on medium-high, then sauté the bacon until it's crisp.
3. Preheat oven to 350 degrees Fahrenheit.
4. Add spinach to the pan with the bacon grease and sauté, stirring, until the spinach is wilted.
5. In a medium bowl, add cream cheese, ½ cup sour cream, 1 ½ tablespoons chopped parsley, and garlic. Season with salt and pepper to taste.
6. Mix to combine, then fold in crumbled bacon.
7. Add the wilted spinach, Parmesan cheese and lemon juice. Mix well.
8. Divide the mixture between three oven-safe ramekins.
9. Bake for 25 minutes, then broil for an additional 3-4 minutes until the top of the dip slightly browned.

Nutrition Information Per Serving:

- Total Fat: 24 grams
- Carbohydrates: 6 grams
- Protein: 10 grams

Keto Hot Wings

Servings: 5
Time Required: 45 minutes

Ingredients:
- 2 lbs. chicken wings
- 1 Tbsp. olive oil
- 1 Tbsp. chili powder
- 1 Tbsp. smoked paprika
- 1 ½ tsp. ground cumin
- 1 tsp. ground cayenne pepper
- 1 ½ tsp. garlic powder
- 1 ½ tsp. onion powder
- 1 ½ tsp. kosher salt
- 1 ½ tsp. black pepper

Directions:
1. Preheat oven to 350 degrees Fahrenheit.
2. Pat wings dry with a paper towel.
3. Place wings in a large bowl and toss with olive oil to coat.
4. Combine all seasonings in a small bowl.
5. Sprinkle half of the seasoning mix onto the chicken wings and rub firmly into the skin of the wings. Flip wings and sprinkle remaining half onto wings and rub in.
6. Place a baking rack in a shallow, foil-lined baking pan with sides. Place seasoned wings on rack.
7. Bake for 20 minutes.
8. After 20 minutes, carefully turn each wing over and bake for 10 more minutes.
9. Turn oven broiler on low and broil for another 10 minutes.

Nutrition Information Per Serving:
- Total Fat: 32 grams
- Carbohydrates: 3.5 grams
- Protein: 34 grams

Bacon Sausage Bites

Servings: 6
Time Required: 45 minutes

Ingredients:
- 24 mini smoked sausage links
- 6 slices bacon
- 3 Tbsp. sugar-free BBQ Sauce
- Salt and pepper to taste

Directions:
1. Preheat oven to 375 degrees Fahrenheit.
2. Cut each slice of bacon into four equal parts. Place a sausage link on top of the slice of bacon.
3. Roll the bacon around the sausage link, overlapping it slightly where the ends meet.
4. Stick a toothpick into the overlapping piece and place on a foil-covered baking sheet. Repeat with the other sausage links.
5. Put baking sheet into the over and bake for 25 minutes.
6. Remove the baking sheet from the oven and, using a basting brush, lightly brush the links with BBQ sauce.
7. Place back in the oven and bake for another 10-12 minutes.
8. Remove from the oven and let cool slightly before serving.

Nutrition Information Per Serving:
- Total Fat: 19 grams
- Carbohydrates: 3 grams
- Protein: 14 grams

Keto Deviled Eggs

Servings: 4
Time Required: 15 minutes

Ingredients:
- 8 eggs
- ¼ cup mayonnaise
- 2 tsp. mustard
- 1 tsp. lemon juice
- 1 tsp. smoked paprika
- Salt and pepper

Directions:
1. Hard boil the eggs, peel and then slice in half lengthwise.
2. Slice in half lengthwise.
3. Carefully remove the egg yolks from the whites. In a medium bowl, use a fork to mash the yolks with mayonnaise, mustard, vinegar, salt and pepper to taste.
4. Carefully spoon the yolk mixture back into the hollows in the egg whited.
5. Sprinkle with smoked paprika.

Nutrition Information Per Serving:
- Total Fat: 20 grams
- Carbohydrates: 0 grams
- Protein: 12 grams

Creamy Squash Soup

Servings: 10
Time Required: About 40 minutes

Ingredients:
- 10 cups butternut squash, cubed
- 1 Tbsp. olive oil
- 1 onion, chopped
- 4 cloves garlic, minced
- 1 ½ tsp. salt
- ½ tsp. black pepper
- 5 cups vegetable stock
- 1 cup heavy cream

Directions:
1. Heat the oil in a heavy skillet over medium-high heat. Add onion, garlic, salt and pepper and sauté, stirring, until the onion is translucent.
2. Add squash and stock to a large pot. Transfer vegetables to the pot.
3. Bring to a low simmer and cook until the squash is tender, about 20-30 minutes. Add water if necessary during cooking.
4. Add the cream, stirring to combine. If you have an immersion blender, use it to puree the soup in the pot. If not, transfer the soup to a blender or food processor and blend to a smooth puree.
5. Serve warm.

Nutrition Information Per Serving:
- Total Fat: 22 grams
- Carbohydrates: 9 grams
- Protein: 3 grams

Cauliflower Cheese Soup

Servings: 4
Time Required: About 40 minutes

Ingredients:
- 1 head cauliflower, chopped
- ½ onion, chopped
- 2 Tbsp. olive oil
- 3 cups chicken stock
- 1 tsp. garlic powder
- 1 tsp. kosher salt
- 4 oz. cream cheese, cubed
- 1 cup cheddar cheese, grated
- ½ cup milk

Directions:
1. Heat the oil in a heavy stock pot over medium-high heat. Add onion and cook until softened, about 3 minutes.
2. Add cauliflower, stock, salt and garlic powder.
3. Bring to a low simmer and cook until the cauliflower is tender, about 20 minutes. Add water if necessary during cooking.
4. Transfer cauliflower to a blender or food processor and blend to a smooth puree.
5. Return pureed cauliflower to the pot and add the cream cheese and cheddar cheese, stirring as the mixture heats over medium-low heat.
6. When the cheese has melted, add the milk and heat thoroughly.

Nutrition Information Per Serving:
- Total Fat: 8 grams
- Carbohydrates: 17 grams
- Protein: 5 grams

Spicy Chicken Cheese Soup

Servings: 4
Time Required: About 30 minutes

Ingredients:

- 2 chicken breasts, boneless and skinless, cooked and cubed
- 3 cups chicken stock
- ½ cup celery, diced
- ¼ cup diced onion
- 1 clove garlic, minced
- 1 Tbsp. butter
- 1 cup heavy cream
- 2 cups cheddar cheese, grated
- 1 Tbsp. ranch dressing mix
- ¼ tsp. red pepper flakes

Directions:

1. Combine all ingredients, excluding the heavy cream and the cheddar cheese, in a heavy stock pot.
2. Bring to a low simmer and cook until the chicken is thoroughly cooked, about 30 minutes. Add water if necessary during cooking.
3. Slowly stir in the cream and cheese, stirring until the cheese is melted.
4. Transfer from the pot to serving bowls and serve hot.

Nutrition Information Per Serving:

- Total Fat: 10 grams
- Carbohydrates: 6 grams
- Protein: 12 grams

Keto Chili

Servings: 10
Time Required: About 50 minutes

Ingredients:
- 2 ½ lbs. ground beef, 85 percent lean
- ½ large white onion, diced
- 8 cloves garlic, minced
- 2 cans (15 oz. each) diced tomatoes, liquid reserved
- 6 oz. tomato paste
- 4 oz. canned green chilis, liquid reserved
- 2 Tbsp. Worcestershire sauce
- ¼ cup chili powder
- 2 Tbsp. cumin
- 1 Tbsp. dried oregano
- 2 tsp. kosher salt
- 1 tsp. freshly ground black pepper
- 1 Tbsp. olive oil

Directions:
1. Heat the oil in a heavy stock pot over medium-high heat. When the oil is hot, add the onions and sauté until soft and translucent, about 5 minutes.
2. Add garlic to the pot and sauté for one minute more.
3. Add ground beef to the pot and sauté until the meat is thoroughly browned, stirring constantly with a wooden spoon or spatula. This should take about 10 minutes.
4. Add the rest of the ingredients to the pot and stir to combine.
5. Bring to a low simmer and cook until fragrant, about 30 minutes. Add water if necessary during cooking.

Nutrition Information Per Serving:
- Total Fat: 18 grams
- Carbohydrates: 13 grams
- Protein: 23 grams

Keto Mexican-Style Soup

Servings: 8-10
Time Required: About 50 minutes

Ingredients:
- 2 lbs. ground beef, 85 percent lean
- ¼ cup onion, diced
- 4 cloves garlic, minced
- 2 Tbsp. chili powder
- 2 tsp. cumin
- 20 oz. canned diced tomatoes
- 4 oz. canned green chilis
- 32 oz. beef stock
- 8 oz. cream cheese
- ½ cup heavy cream
- 1 Tbsp. olive oil

Directions:
1. Heat the oil in a heavy stock pot over medium-high heat. When the oil is hot, add the onions to the pot and sauté until soft and translucent, about 5 minutes.
2. Add garlic to the pot and sauté for one minute more.
3. Add ground beef to the pot and sauté until the meat is thoroughly browned, stirring constantly with a wooden spoon or spatula. This should take about 10 minutes.
4. Add the rest of the ingredients, excluding the cream and cream cheese, to the pot and stir to combine.
5. Bring to a low simmer and cook until fragrant, about 30 minutes. Add water if necessary during cooking.
6. Stir in cream and cream cheese, stirring constantly until cream cheese is melted and soup is thick and creamy.
7. Transfer to serving bowls and serve hot.

Nutrition Information Per Serving:
- Total Fat: 28 grams
- Carbohydrates: 8 grams
- Protein: 27 grams

Keto Chinese-Style Soup

Servings: 8-10
Time Required: About 40 minutes

Ingredients:
- 5 cups chicken stock
- 1 lb. pork tenderloin or other lean pork, sliced into thin bite-sized pieces
- 1 cup fresh mushrooms, chopped
- 3 Tbsp. soy sauce
- 1 Tbsp. white vinegar
- 2 Tbsp. rice vinegar
- 1 tsp. salt
- 2 tsp. freshly ground black pepper
- 3 Tbsp. water
- 4 eggs, beaten
- 1 lb. tofu, extra firm, cubed

Directions:
1. Put all ingredients, excluding eggs and tofu, in a heavy stock pot.
2. Bring to a low simmer and cook until the meat is thoroughly cooked and the mushrooms are tender, about 30 minutes. Add water if necessary during cooking.
3. Slowly and carefully stir in the tofu and beaten eggs. Allow the warm soup to sit for at least 3 minute to allow the eggs to cook.
4. Transfer to serving bowls and serve hot.

Nutrition Information Per Serving:
- Total Fat: 5 grams
- Carbohydrates: 5 grams
- Protein: 20 grams

Spicy Pork Soup

Servings: 8-10
Time Required: About 40 minutes

Ingredients:
- 1 lb. pork shoulder, cut into bite-size pieces
- 2 Tbsp. soy sauce
- 2 Tbsp. rice vinegar
- 2 tsp. Thai chili peppers, chopped
- 1 tsp. salt
- 6 cloves garlic, minced
- 3-inch piece of fresh ginger, peeled and minced
- ½ onion, sliced
- 2 Tbsp. olive oil
- 2 Tbsp. black bean paste
- 3 cups water

Directions:
1. Heat the oil in a heavy stock pot over medium-high heat. When the oil is hot, add the ginger and garlic, and sauté until fragrant, about a minute.
2. Add all the other ingredients to the pot, stirring to combine.
3. Bring to a low simmer and cook until the meat is thoroughly cooked and the peppers are tender, about 30 minutes. Add water if necessary during cooking.
4. Transfer the soup to serving bowls and serve hot, garnished with chopped fresh cilantro.

Nutrition Information Per Serving:
- Total Fat: 8 grams
- Carbohydrates: 7 grams
- Protein: 10 grams

Creamy Keto Broccoli Cheese Soup

Servings: 8-10
Time Required: About 40 minutes

Ingredients:
- 1 cup broccoli, chopped
- 5 oz. cheddar cheese, grated
- 2 Tbsp. butter
- ¼ cup onion, diced
- ¼ cup celery, diced
- 1 ½ cups chicken stock
- ½ cup heavy cream
- 1 Tbsp. olive oil

Directions:
1. Heat the oil in a heavy stock pot over medium-high heat. When the oil is hot, add the onions and celery to the pot and sauté until the onion is soft and translucent, about 5 minutes.
2. Add garlic to the pot and sauté for one minute more.
3. Add the rest of the ingredients, excluding the cream and cheese, to the pot and stir to combine.
4. Bring to a low simmer and cook until the vegetables are tender, about 30 minutes. Add water if necessary during cooking.
5. Stir in cream, stirring constantly until the cheese is melted and soup is thick and creamy.
6. Transfer to serving bowls and serve hot.

Nutrition Information Per Serving:
- Total Fat: 36 grams
- Carbohydrates: 5 grams
- Protein: 13 grams

Keto Yellow Curry

Servings: 6-8
Time Required: About 40 minutes

Ingredients:

- 4 chicken thighs, skinless boneless, cut into bite-sized pieces
- 14.5-oz. can unsweetened coconut milk, full fat
- 2 tsp. Thai yellow curry paste
- 2 tsp. fish sauce
- 3 tsp. soy sauce
- 1 tsp. honey
- 2 green onion chopped
- 4 cloves garlic, minced
- 2 Tbsp. fresh ginger, minced
- ¼ cup fresh cilantro, chopped
- ¼ cup spring onions, chopped

Directions:

1. Place chicken, coconut milk, curry paste, fish sauce, soy sauce and honey into a heavy stock pot.
2. Bring to a low simmer and cook until the chicken is thoroughly cooked and the spices are fragrant, about 30 minutes. Add water if necessary during cooking.
3. Transfer to serving bowls and garnish with cilantro and spring onions.
4. Serve hot.

Nutrition Information Per Serving:

- Total Fat: 29 grams
- Carbohydrates: 9 grams
- Protein: 14 grams

Sausage Kale Soup

Servings: 6-8
Time Required: About 40 minutes

Ingredients:
- 4 cups fresh kale, chopped
- ½ lb. smoked sausage, sliced into ½-inch-thick slices
- ½ cup canned white beans
- 2 cloves garlic, minced
- ½ onion, diced
- ½ cup celery, diced
- ¼ tsp. freshly ground black pepper
- Salt to taste
- 1 cup water

Directions:
1. Place all ingredients into a heavy stock pot.
2. Bring to a low simmer and cook until fragrant, about 30 minutes. Add water if necessary during cooking.
3. Transfer the soup to serving bowls and serve hot.

Nutrition Information Per Serving:
- Total Fat: 15 grams
- Carbohydrates: 15 grams
- Protein: 9 grams

Hungarian-Style Stew

Servings: 8-10
Time Required: About 40 minutes

Ingredients:
- 1 Tbsp. olive oil
- ½ onion, diced
- 2 cloves of garlic, minced
- 1 lb. ground beef roast, 90 percent lean
- ¼ cup button mushrooms, chopped
- 1 bell pepper, chopped
- ½ cup beef stock
- 1 Tbsp. smoked paprika
- ¼ cup fresh tomatoes, diced
- Salt and pepper to taste

Directions:
1. Heat the oil in a heavy stock pot over medium-high heat. When the oil is hot, add the onions to the pot and sauté until soft and translucent, about 5 minutes.
2. Add garlic to the pot and sauté for one minute more.
3. Add ground beef to the pot and sauté until the meat is thoroughly browned, stirring constantly with a wooden spoon or spatula. This should take about 10 minutes.
4. Add the rest of the ingredients to the pot and stir to combine.
5. Bring to a low simmer and cook until fragrant, about 30 minutes. Add water if necessary during cooking.
6. Transfer the stew to serving bowls and serve hot garnished with chopped fresh parsley.

Nutrition Information Per Serving:
- Total Fat: 38 grams
- Carbohydrates: 6 grams
- Protein: 20 grams

Creamy Jalapeno Chicken Soup

Servings: 8-10
Time Required: About 45 minutes

Ingredients:
- 1 lb. boneless skinless chicken breasts, cubed
- 3 Tbsp. butter
- 2 cloves garlic, minced
- ½ onion, chopped
- ½ bell pepper, chopped
- 2 jalapeno peppers, seeded and chopped
- ½ lb. bacon, cooked crisp and crumbled
- 6 oz. cream cheese
- 3 cups chicken stock
- ½ cup heavy cream
- ¼ tsp. paprika
- 1 tsp. cumin
- 1 tsp. salt
- ½ tsp. freshly ground black pepper

Directions:
1. Heat the oil in a heavy stock pot over medium-high heat. When the butter is melted, add onion, bell pepper and jalapenos and sauté until the onion is soft, about 5 minutes.
2. Add the stock, chicken and cream cheese to the pot, stirring to combine.
3. Bring to a low simmer and cook until the chicken is thoroughly cooked and the vegetables are tender, about 30 minutes. Add water if necessary during cooking.
4. Stir in the cream and crumbled bacon, stirring to combine.
5. Transfer to serving bowls and serve hot topped with grated cheese.

Nutrition Information Per Serving:
- Total Fat: 40 grams
- Carbohydrates: 4 grams
- Protein: 41 grams

Louisiana Pork Stew

Servings: 8-10
Time Required: About 40 minutes

Ingredients:
- 1 onion, chopped
- 4 cloves garlic, minced
- 14 oz. canned diced tomatoes
- 5 oz. canned green chilis
- 3 cups chicken stock
- 1 tsp. dried thyme
- 2 tsp. Cajun seasoning
- 1 lb. pork butt, cubed
- ½ cup heavy whipping cream
- 5 cups baby spinach, chopped

Directions:
1. Combine all ingredients except the cream and spinach in large stock pot.
2. Bring to a low simmer and cook until the meat is thoroughly cooked and the soup is fragrant, about 30 minutes. Add water if necessary during cooking.
3. Stir in the cream, then add the spinach. Cook until the spinach is wilted.
4. Transfer to serving bowls and serve hot.

Nutrition Information Per Serving:
- Total Fat: 17 grams
- Carbohydrates: 9 grams
- Protein: 23 grams

Chinese Chicken Soup

Servings: 8-10
Time Required: About 40 minutes

Ingredients:
- ¼ cup sesame oil
- 6 dried red Thai chilis
- 5 cloves garlic, crushed
- 2 Tbsp. fresh ginger, peeled and sliced
- 2 lbs. boneless skinless chicken thighs, chopped
- 3 cups chicken stock
- ¼ cup soy sauce
- ¼ cup dry sherry
- Salt to taste
- ¼ cup fresh Thai basil, chopped

Directions:
1. Heat the oil in a heavy stock pot over medium-high heat. Add the garlic, chilis and ginger to the pot and sauté just until fragrant, about a minute.
2. Lower the heat and add all the other ingredients, excluding the basil, to the pot.
3. Bring to a low simmer and cook until the chicken is thoroughly cooked and the soup is fragrant, about 30 minutes. Add water if necessary during cooking.
4. Bring the soup to a boil again and stir in the basil, stirring until the basil is fragrant and wilted.
5. Transfer to serving bowls and serve hot.

Nutrition Information Per Serving:
- Total Fat: 15 grams
- Carbohydrates: 7 grams
- Protein: 31 grams

Mushroom Chicken Soup

Servings: 8-10
Time Required: About 40 minutes

Ingredients:
- 1 onion, chopped
- 3 cloves garlic, minced
- 2 cups fresh button mushrooms, chopped
- 1 medium yellow summer squash, chopped
- 1 lb. chicken breast, boneless and skinless, cubed
- 3 cups chicken stock
- Salt and pepper to taste
- 1 tsp. poultry seasoning

Directions:
1. Add all ingredients to a heavy stock pot.
2. Bring to a low simmer and cook until the chicken is thoroughly cooked and the soup is fragrant, about 30 minutes. Add water if necessary during cooking.
3. Transfer soup to serving bowls and serve hot.

Nutrition Information Per Serving:
- Total Fat: 15 grams
- Carbohydrates: 9 grams
- Protein: 30 grams

Mexican-Style Beef Stew

Servings: 6-8
Time Required: About 40 minutes

Ingredients:
- 1 lb. beef chuck steak, cut into large pieces
- 1 onion, chopped
- 1 bell pepper, chopped
- 6 cloves garlic, minced
- 2 cups canned diced tomatoes
- 2 cups chicken stock
- 1 tsp. ground cumin
- 1 tsp. salt
- 1 tsp. smoked paprika
- ½ tsp. red pepper flakes
- ½ tsp. oregano

Directions:
1. Put all the ingredients in a heavy stock pot.
2. Bring to a low simmer and cook until the meat is thoroughly cooked and the soup is fragrant, about 30 minutes. Add water if necessary during cooking.
3. Remove the meat from the sauce and allow it to cool slightly.
4. Pull the meat apart into bite-size pieces and return to the sauce. Stir over medium-low heat to heat through.
5. Serve hot with steamed or riced cauliflower.

Nutrition Information Per Serving:
- Total Fat: 13 grams
- Carbohydrates: 11 grams
- Protein: 16 grams

Vietnamese-Style Stew

Servings: 6-8
Time Required: About 40 minutes

Ingredients:
- 1 lb. beef stew meat
- 1 onion, diced
- 2 Tbsp. tomato paste
- 2 whole star anise
- 1 Tbsp. fresh ginger, peeled and minced
- 3 cloves garlic, minced
- 6 cups water
- 1 tsp. ground pepper
- ½ tsp. Chinese five-spice
- ½ tsp. curry powder
- 2 carrots, peeled and sliced

Directions:
1. Place all ingredients in a heavy stock pot.
2. Bring to a low simmer and cook until the meat is thoroughly cooked and the soup is fragrant, about 30 minutes. Add water if necessary during cooking.
3. Serve the stew hot.

Nutrition Information Per Serving:
- Total Fat: 9 grams
- Carbohydrates: 8 grams
- Protein: 15 grams

Chinese-Style Chicken Soup

Servings: 6-8
Time Required: About 70 minutes

Ingredients:
- 1 lb. chicken breast, boneless and skinless, cut into bite-size pieces
- 1 Tbsp. peanut butter
- 1 Tbsp. black bean paste
- 2 tsp. soy sauce
- 2 tsp. rice wine vinegar
- ½ tsp. freshly ground black pepper
- ¼ cup water

Directions:
1. In a medium bowl, combine peanut butter, bean paste, soy sauce, vinegar, pepper and water.
2. Add chicken and toss to coat. Allow the chicken to marinate for 30 minutes.
3. Put everything into a heavy stock pot, along with another 3 cups water.
4. Bring to a low simmer and cook until the chicken is thoroughly cooked and the soup is fragrant, about 30 minutes. Add water if necessary during cooking.
5. Transfer to serving bowls and serve garnished with chopped fresh cilantro.

Nutrition Information Per Serving:
- Total Fat: 7 grams
- Carbohydrates: 7 grams
- Protein: 22 grams

Green Chili Chicken Soup

Servings: 6-8
Time Required: About 2 hours

Ingredients:
- ½ cup dry navy beans, soaked for an hour in hot water
- 1 onion diced
- 3 New Mexico green chili peppers, chopped
- 5 cloves garlic, minced
- 1 cup cauliflower, diced
- 1 lb. chicken breast, boneless and skinless, cut into bite-size pieces
- 4 cups chicken stock
- ¼ cup fresh cilantro, chopped
- 1 tsp. ground coriander
- 1 tsp. ground cumin
- 1 tsp. salt
- 2 oz. cream cheese

Directions:
1. Put all the ingredients, excluding the cream cheese, into a large heavy stock pot.
2. Bring to a low simmer and cook until the beans are tender, about 60 minutes. Add water if necessary during cooking.
3. Transfer the chicken to a plate and set aside.
4. Using an immersion blender, blend the soup until it is smooth.
5. Return the soup to a simmer.
6. When the soup is bubbly, stir in the cream cheese until it's melted.
7. Return the chicken to the soup and stir until everything is heated through.
8. Transfer the soup to serving bowls and serve hot.

Nutrition Information Per Serving:
- Total Fat: 5 grams
- Carbohydrates: 13 grams
- Protein: 22 grams

Red Chili

Servings: 6-8
Time Required: About 35 minutes

Ingredients:
- 3 tsp. chili powder
- 2 tsp. ground cumin
- 2 tsp. salt
- 1 tsp. dried oregano
- 1 Tbsp. olive oil
- 1 onion, chopped
- 2 cloves garlic, minced
- 1 lb. ground beef, 90 percent lean
- 1 cup canned diced tomatoes
- 1 Tbsp. canned chipotle chilis, chopped
- 2 corn tortillas, torn into small pieces
- ½ cup water

Directions:
1. In a small bowl, mix chili powder, cumin, salt and oregano.
2. In a blender or food processor, blend tomatoes, chilis, and tortilla pieces until smooth.
3. Heat the oil in a heavy stock pot over medium-high heat. When the oil is hot, sauté the onions until they're softened, about 3 minutes. Add the garlic and sauté for about a minute more.
4. Add the ground beef to the pot and sauté until it's well browned and broken up.
5. Stir in the spice mixture and sauté until fragrant, about 30 seconds.
6. Add the tomato/tortilla mixture to the pot, along with 2 cups water.
7. Bring to a low simmer and cook until fragrant about 20 minutes. Add water if necessary during cooking.
8. Transfer the chili to serving bowls and serve hot.

Nutrition Information Per Serving:
- Total Fat: 24 grams
- Carbohydrates: 12 grams
- Protein: 30 grams

Green Chili

Servings: 6-8
Time Required: About 30 minutes

Ingredients:
- 2 lbs. pork butt, cut into large pieces
- 3 tomatillos, sliced
- 3 jalapeno peppers, seeded and chopped
- 2 New Mexico green chili peppers, seeded and chopped
- 6 cloves garlic, minced
- 1 tomato, chopped
- 3 cups chicken stock
- 2 tsp. cumin
- Salt and pepper to taste

Directions:
1. Put the tomatillos, jalapenos, New Mexico chilis, garlic, chicken stock and tomato into a heavy stock pot.
2. Put the pork pieces on top of the vegetables in the pot.
3. Add the cumin, salt, and pepper on top of the meat.
4. Bring to a low simmer and cook until fragrant, about 20 minutes. Add water if necessary during cooking.
5. Carefully remove the pieces of meat and set aside on a plate.
6. Using an immersion blender, blend the sauce in the pot until it's smooth.
7. Return the pork to the pot and stir to combine.
8. Transfer the chili to serving bowls and serve hot, garnished with chopped fresh cilantro.

Nutrition Information Per Serving:
- Total Fat: 4 grams
- Carbohydrates: 4 grams
- Protein: 26 grams

Tortilla Soup

Servings: 6-8
Time Required: About 30 minutes

Ingredients:
- 1 lb. chicken breast, boneless and skinless
- 2 corn tortillas, torn into pieces
- ½ onion, chopped
- 1 cup tomatoes, chopped
- 2 cloves garlic
- 1 Tbsp. canned chipotle chili in adobo sauce, chopped
- ½ jalapeno pepper
- ¼ cup fresh cilantro, chopped
- 1 tsp. salt
- 1 Tbsp. olive oil
- 4 cups water

Directions:
1. In a blender or food processor, combine onion, tomatoes, garlic, chipotle, jalapeno and cilantro. Blend until the mixture is smooth.
2. Heat the oil in a heavy stock pot over medium-high heat. When the oil is hot, add the blended mixture to the pot. Cook, stirring, until fragrant, about a minute or two.
3. Add the tortillas, chicken, and water to the pot.
4. Bring to a low simmer and cook until chicken is cooked, about 20 minutes. Add water if necessary during cooking.
5. Remove the chicken from the pot and set aside to cool slightly. When it is cool enough to handle, shred it with a fork or your fingers.
6. Return the chicken to the pot. Allow the soup to reheat, then transfer to serving bowls and serve hot.

Nutrition Information Per Serving:
- Total Fat: 5 grams
- Carbohydrates: 5 grams
- Protein: 12 grams

Keto Vegetable Soup

Servings: 6-8
Time Required: About 45 minutes

Ingredients:
- 1 turnip, cut into bite-size pieces
- 1 onion, chopped
- 6 stalks celery, diced
- 1 carrot, sliced
- 15 oz. pumpkin puree
- 1 lb. green beans frozen or fresh
- 8 cups chicken stock
- 2 cups water
- 1 Tbsp. fresh basil, chopped
- ¼ tsp. thyme leaves
- 1/8 tsp. rubbed sage
- Salt to taste
- 1 lb. fresh spinach, chopped

Directions:
1. Put all the ingredients, excluding the spinach, into a heavy stock pot.
2. Bring to a low simmer and cook until the vegetables are tender, about 30 minutes. Add water if necessary during cooking.
3. Add the spinach and stir until it's wilted, about 5 minutes.
4. Transfer to serving bowls and serve hot.

Nutrition Information Per Serving:
- Total Fat: 0 grams
- Carbohydrates: 10 grams
- Protein: 3 grams

Keto Cabbage Soup

Servings: 6-8
Time Required: About 45 minutes

Ingredients:
- 2 lbs. ground beef, 90 percent lean
- ¼ cup onion, diced
- 1 clove garlic, minced
- 1 tsp. cumin
- 1 head cabbage, chopped
- 4 cubes bouillon
- 1 ¼ cup canned diced tomatoes
- 5 oz. canned green chilis
- 4 cups beef stock
- Salt and pepper to taste

Directions:
1. Heat a heavy stock pot over medium-high heat. When the pot is hot, add the ground beef and brown the meat, stirring to break it up as it browns. This should take about 10 minutes.
2. When the meat is browned, add the onions and sauté for 5-7 minutes more. Add the garlic and sauté for one more minute.
3. Bring to a low simmer and cook until the vegetables are tender, about 30 minutes. Add water if necessary during cooking.
4. Transfer to serving bowls and serve hot.

Nutrition Information Per Serving:
- Total Fat: 18 grams
- Carbohydrates: 6 grams
- Protein: 17 grams

Bone Broth

Servings: 6-8
Time Required: About 2 hours

Ingredients:

- 4 lbs. chicken parts, including bones, skin and/or fat
- 1 onion, chopped
- 2 carrots, chopped
- 2 stalks celery, chopped
- 2 cloves garlic, peeled and chopped
- 6 sprigs fresh parsley
- 1 Tbsp. cider vinegar
- 1 tsp. sea salt
- 4 quarts water

Directions:

1. Add all the ingredients to a heavy stock pot.
2. Cover and bring to a low simmer for about 2 hours. Add water if necessary during cooking.
3. Very carefully use a strainer to remove the solids from the stock.
4. Transfer the broth to clean jars and refrigerate. The broth will keep in the refrigerator for up to 5 days, or you can freeze it in freezer-safe containers for up to 3 months.

Meats

A keto diet relies on meats and poultry to provide the fats and protein that you need to fuel ketosis. These recipes will help you to find new, delicious ways to prepare these staples of the diet.

Pressure Cooker Spicy Mocha Beef Roast

Servings: 4
Time Required: About 45 minutes

Ingredients:
- 2 Tbsp. ground coffee
- 1 Tbsp. black pepper
- 1 Tbsp. cocoa powder
- 1 tsp. red chili flakes
- 1 tsp. chili powder
- 1 tsp. ground ginger
- 1 tsp. kosher salt
- 2 lbs. beef chuck roast, cubed
- 2 cups beef stock
- 1 onion, chopped
- 3 Tbsp. balsamic vinegar
- Salt and pepper to taste

Directions:
1. In a small bowl, combine ground coffee, black pepper, cocoa powder, chili flakes, chili powder, ginger and kosher salt.
2. In a medium bowl, toss cubed beef with the 3 tablespoons of the spice mixture until the meat is well coated.
3. Place the meat in an electronic pressure cooker, and add the stock, onion and vinegar.
4. Set the cooking time for 35 minutes.
5. At the end of the cooking time, allow the pot to vent naturally.
6. When the pressure is fully released, remove the lid.
7. Serve the meat drizzled with the sauce from the pot.

Nutrition Information Per Serving:

- Total Fat: 10 grams
- Carbohydrates: 16 grams
- Protein: 48 grams

Keto Meatballs

Servings: 3-5
Time Required: About 30 minutes

Ingredients:

- 1 ½ lbs. ground beef (85 per cent lean)
- 2 eggs
- ¾ cup parmesan cheese, grated
- ¼ tsp. garlic powder
- ¼ tsp. onion powder
- ¼ tsp. oregano
- 1 tsp. kosher salt
- 2 Tbsp. chopped fresh parsley
- 3 cups sugar-free marinara sauce

Directions:

1. In a medium mixing bowl, combine ground beef and seasonings by hand until thoroughly mixed.
2. Form into meatballs about 2 inches in diameter. You should get 12-15 meatballs.
3. Spray a stock pot lightly with olive oil spray and heat over medium-high heat.
4. Press the sauté button and brown the meatballs, turning to brown them on all sides.
5. Arrange the meatballs in the pot so that they are about a half inch apart. Pour sauce over meatballs.
6. Cover the pot and cook over low heat for 20 minutes.
7. Remove the meatballs and sauce. Serve on their own or over cooked spaghetti squash.

Nutrition Information Per Serving (3 meatballs):

- Total Fat: 33 grams
- Carbohydrates: 5 grams
- Protein: 34 grams

Beef Stroganoff

Servings: 4
Time Required: About 30 minutes

Ingredients:
- 1 Tbsp. olive oil
- ½ onion, chopped
- 1 clove garlic, minced
- 1 lb. beef stew meat
- 1 cup fresh mushrooms, chopped
- 1 Tbsp. Worcestershire sauce
- 1 tsp. salt
- ½ tsp. freshly ground black pepper
- 1 cup water
- ½ cup sour cream

Directions:
1. Heat the oil over medium-high heat in a heavy stock pot. When the oil is hot, add the onions to the pot and sauté until soft and translucent, about 5 minutes.
2. Add garlic to the pot and sauté for one minute more.
3. Add the beef to the pot and sauté until the meat is thoroughly browned on all sides, stirring constantly with a wooden spoon or spatula. This should take about 10 minutes.
4. Add the rest of the ingredients, excluding the sour cream, to the pot and stir to combine.
5. Bring to simmer and cook until beef is thoroughly cooked, about 30 minutes. Add water during cooking if necessary.
6. Stir in the sour cream until it's thoroughly combined.
7. Serve hot over steamed cauliflower.

Nutrition Information Per Serving:
- Total Fat: 16 grams
- Carbohydrates: 9 grams
- Protein: 33 grams

Herbed Beef Roast

Servings: 8-10
Time Required: About 2 hours

Ingredients:
- 3 lb. beef chuck roast
- 3 cloves garlic, minced
- 1 Tbsp. olive oil
- 1 tsp. salt
- ½ tsp. freshly ground black pepper
- ½ tsp. dried rosemary
- 1 Tbsp. butter
- ½ tsp. dried thyme
- ¼ cup balsamic vinegar
- 1 cup beef stock

Directions:
1. In a small bowl, combine salt, pepper, rosemary and thyme. Rub the herb mixture on all sides of the roast.
2. Heat oil in a heavy pot over medium-high heat. When the oil is hot, carefully place the roast into the pot and brown, turning it to evenly brown all sides.
3. Remove the roast from the pot and set aside.
4. Add the butter, vinegar, garlic and stock to the pot, stirring and scraping all the browned bits from the bottom of the pot.
5. Return the roast to the pot.
6. Cover and bring to a simmer. Cook until meat is tender, about 1-1 ½ hours. Add more water if necessary during the cooking process.
7. Serve hot.

Nutrition Information Per Serving:
- Total Fat: 34 grams
- Carbohydrates: 3 grams
- Protein: 60 grams

Asian-Style Ribs

Servings: 4-6
Time Required: About 2 hours

Ingredients:

- 1 ½ lbs. pork spareribs, cut into serving-size pieces
- 1 Tbsp. olive oil
- 1 clove garlic, minced
- 1 Tbsp. fresh ginger, peeled and minced
- 2 Tbsp. black bean sauce
- 1 Tbsp. wine vinegar
- 1 Tbsp. soy sauce
- 1 Tbsp. honey
- 1 cup water
- ½ cup spring onions, chopped

Directions:

1. Heat oil in a heavy pot over medium-high heat. When the oil is hot, sauté the garlic and ginger just until fragrant, about 30 seconds.
2. Add bean sauce, vinegar, soy sauce, honey and water to the pot, stirring to combine.
3. Add ribs to the pot and turn to coat them with the sauce.
4. Cover and bring to a simmer. Cook until meat is tender, about 1-1 ½ hours. Add more water if necessary during the cooking process.
5. Remove the ribs with tongs or a slotted spoon and serve garnished with chopped spring onions.

Nutrition Information Per Serving:

- Total Fat: 32 grams
- Carbohydrates: 5 grams
- Protein: 19 grams

Spicy Lamb

Servings: 4-6
Time Required: About 2 hours

Ingredients:
- 1 lb. leg of lamb, cubed
- 1 cup onion, diced
- 4 cloves garlic, minced
- 2 tsp. fresh ginger, peeled and minced
- 2 tsp. garam masala
- 1 tsp. smoked paprika
- 1 tsp. salt
- 1 tsp. turmeric
- ½ tsp. ground cinnamon
- ¼ tsp. cayenne pepper
- ¼ cup yogurt
- 1 Tbsp. tomato paste
- ¼ cup fresh cilantro, chopped

Directions:
1. Combine all ingredients in a mixing bowl, stirring until lamb is thoroughly coated with the yogurt-spice mixture.
2. Cover the bowl with plastic wrap and refrigerate for at least an hour.
3. After the meat has had a chance to marinate, transfer everything to a heavy pot.
4. Cover and bring to a simmer. Cook until meat is tender, about an hour. Add more water if necessary during the cooking process.
5. Serve the meat hot alone or over steamed cauliflower.

Nutrition Information Per Serving:
- Total Fat: 3 grams
- Carbohydrates: 6 grams
- Protein: 16 grams

Ham and Collard Greens

Servings: 4-6
Time Required: About 45 minutes

Ingredients:
- 6 cups collard greens, chopped
- 2 cups cooked ham, diced
- 1 onion, diced
- 6 cloves garlic, minced
- 1 tsp. salt
- 1 tsp. freshly ground black pepper
- ¼ cup water
- ½ tsp. red pepper flakes
- 1 tsp. dried thyme
- 1 Tbsp. cider vinegar
- 1 tsp. red chili hot sauce

Directions:
1. Place all ingredients except vinegar and hot sauce in a heavy pot.
2. Bring to a simmer. Cook until everything is fragrant, about 30 minutes. Add more water if necessary during the cooking process.
3. Stir in vinegar and hot sauce.
4. Serve hot.

Nutrition Information Per Serving:
- Total Fat: 2 grams
- Carbohydrates: 9 grams
- Protein: 4 grams

Pressure Cooker Pork Chops

Servings: 4
Time Required: About 45 minutes

Ingredients:
- 4 pork loin chops, boneless
- 1 Tbsp. paprika
- 1 tsp. garlic powder
- 1 tsp. onion powder
- 1 tsp. freshly ground black pepper
- 1 tsp. salt
- ¼ tsp. cayenne pepper
- 1 Tbsp. olive oil
- ½ onion, chopped
- 6 oz. button mushrooms, sliced
- 1 Tbsp. butter
- ½ cup heavy cream

Directions:
1. In a small bowl, combine paprika, garlic powder, onion powder, black pepper, salt and cayenne pepper.
2. Rub both sides of the pork chops with 1 tablespoon of the spice mixture.
3. Press the Sauté button on the pot and add oil. When the oil is hot, sauté the pork chops to brown them on both sides, about 3 minutes per side. Remove the chops from the pot and set aside.
4. Stop the Sauté cycle.
5. Add the onions and mushrooms to the pot.
6. Place the pork chops back into the pot on top of the onions and mushrooms.
7. Cover and lock the pot.
8. Set the cook time for 25 minutes and start the cook cycle.
9. At the end of the cooking time, carefully vent the pot manually.
10. Remove the cover and transfer the pork chops to a serving platter.
11. Press the Sauté button on the cooker's control panel.
12. Stir in butter and cream and heat, stirring, for about 5 minutes until the butter is melted.
13. Drizzle the sauce over the pork chops and serve.

Nutrition Information Per Serving:

- Total Fat: 32 grams
- Carbohydrates: 7 grams
- Protein: 40 grams

Slow Cooker Brisket

Servings: 6-8
Time Required: 8-10 hours

Ingredients:
- 2 lbs. beef brisket
- ½ Tbsp. salt
- 2 tsp. freshly ground black pepper
- 2 onions, chopped
- ½ cup water
- 2 Tbsp. tomato paste
- 2 Tbsp. Worcestershire sauce

Directions:
1. Place onions in the bottom of a slow cooker. Place the brisket on top of the onions.
2. In a small bowl, whisk together water, tomato paste and Worcestershire sauce. Pour the mixture over the brisket.
3. Cover the slow cooker and cook on low for 8-10 hours.
4. Transfer the brisket to a serving platter, topped with sauce from the pot.

Nutrition Information Per Serving:
- Total Fat: 8 grams
- Carbohydrates: 5 grams
- Protein: 24 grams

Slow Cooker Curry Beef

Servings: 6
Time Required: 6-8 hours

Ingredients:
- 1 ½ lbs. beef stew meat
- 1 onion, chopped
- 2 tomatoes, chopped
- 4 cloves garlic
- ½ cup fresh cilantro, chopped
- 1 tsp. cumin
- ½ tsp. coriander
- 1 tsp. garam masala
- ½ tsp. cayenne pepper
- Salt to taste

Directions:
1. In a blender or food processor, blend the onion, tomatoes, garlic, cilantro, cumin, coriander, garam masala, cayenne, and salt to a smooth puree.
2. Put the meat into the slow cooker, and then pour the vegetable puree over the top of the meat.
3. Cover the pot and cook on the low setting for 6-8 hours.
4. Serve the curry hot over riced cauliflower, garnished with chopped fresh cilantro.

Nutrition Information Per Serving:
- Total Fat: 8 grams
- Carbohydrates: 4 grams
- Protein: 31 grams

One-Pot Shawarma

Servings: 6
Time Required: About 45 minutes

Ingredients:
- 2 tsp. dried oregano
- 1 tsp. ground cinnamon
- ½ tsp. ground allspice
- ½ tsp. cayenne pepper
- 1 tsp. ground cumin
- 1 tsp. ground coriander
- 1 tsp. salt
- 1 lb. ground beef, 90 percent lean
- 1 onion, sliced
- 1 red bell pepper, chopped
- 2 cups cabbage, chopped
- 1 cup chicken stock

Directions:
1. In a small bowl, mix oregano, cinnamon, allspice, cayenne, cumin, coriander, and salt.
2. Heat a heavy stock pot over medium-high heat. When the pot is hot, add the ground beef. Sauté, stirring, until the meat is thoroughly browned.
3. When the meat is well browned, add 2 tablespoons of the spice mixture and stir to combine.
4. Add the onions, bell pepper, stock and cabbage.
5. Bring to a simmer. Cook until vegetables are tender, about 30 minutes. Add more water if necessary during the cooking process.
6. At the end of the cooking time, allow the pot to vent naturally for 5 minutes. After 5 minutes, carefully release any remaining pressure and uncover the pot.
7. Serve the shawarma hot.

Nutrition Information Per Serving:
- Total Fat: 5 grams
- Carbohydrates: 8 grams
- Protein: 25 grams

Easy Beef Stew

Servings: 6
Time Required: About 45 minutes

Ingredients:

- 1 lb. ground beef, 90 percent lean
- 5 oz. canned tomato sauce
- 2 Tbsp. tomato paste
- 2 cups frozen sweet corn
- 1 cup frozen carrots
- 3 Tbsp. cider vinegar
- 1 Tbsp. soy sauce
- 1 tsp. salt
- 2 tsp. freshly ground black pepper

Directions:

1. Heat a heavy stock pot over medium-high heat. When the pot is hot, add the ground beef. Sauté, stirring, until the meat is thoroughly browned.
2. When the meat is well browned, add the rest of the ingredients, plus 2 cups water.
3. Bring to a simmer. Cook until vegetables are tender, about 30 minutes. Add more water if necessary during the cooking process.
4. Serve the stew hot, garnished with chopped fresh parsley.

Nutrition Information Per Serving:

- Total Fat: 4 grams
- Carbohydrates: 20 grams
- Protein: 19 grams

Barbecue-Style Ribs

Servings: 6
Time Required: About 3 hours

Ingredients:
- 1 tsp. dried oregano
- 1 tsp. garlic powder
- 1 tsp. onion powder
- ½ tsp. smoked paprika
- ½ tsp. dry mustard
- ¼ tsp. cayenne powder
- ½ tsp. salt
- ¼ tsp. freshly ground black pepper
- 2 lbs. pork baby back ribs, cut into serving-size pieces

Directions:
1. Heat oven to 325 degrees Fahrenheit.
2. In a small bowl, mix oregano, garlic powder, onion powder, paprika, mustard, cayenne, salt and pepper.
3. Rub the ribs thoroughly on all sides with the spice mixture.
4. Wrap the ribs loosely in aluminum foil, making sure that the foil is sealed on all sides.
5. Place the foil-wrapped ribs on a baking sheet, and put the sheet on the center rack of the oven.
6. Bake until the ribs are very tender, about 3 hours.
7. Remove the foil and place the ribs under a hot broiler to brown them, about 2 minutes per side.

Nutrition Information Per Serving:
- Total Fat: 40 grams
- Carbohydrates: 1 gram
- Protein: 65 grams

Slow Cooker Carne Adovada

Servings: 6
Time Required: About 6-8 hours

Ingredients:
- 2 lbs. pork shoulder, cut into bite-size pieces
- ¼ cup soy sauce
- 1 tsp. olive oil
- 1 onion, chopped
- 3 cloves garlic, minced
- 1 tsp. salt
- 1 tsp. oregano
- 1 Tbsp. cider vinegar
- 1 can chipotle chilis in adobo sauce
- ¼ cup chili powder

Directions:
1. In a blender or food processor, combine onion, garlic, salt, oregano , chipotles, vinegar, soy sauce, and chili powder. Blend until the mixture is a smooth puree.
2. Put the pork into the slow cooker. Pour the seasoning mixture over the pork. Use ¼ cup water to rinse the blender jar, and add the water to the pot, too.
3. Cook at the low setting for 6-8 hours.
4. Uncover the pot and transfer the meat with its sauce to a serving platter and serve hot.

Nutrition Information Per Serving:
- Total Fat: 5 grams
- Carbohydrates: 5 grams
- Protein: 14 grams

Keto Lasagna

Servings: 6
Time Required: About 1 hour

Ingredients:
- 1 lb. ground beef, 90 percent lean
- 2 cloves garlic, minced
- 1 onion, chopped
- 1 ½ cups ricotta cheese
- ½ cup Parmesan cheese
- 1 egg
- 25 oz. jarred marinara sauce
- 8 oz. mozzarella cheese, sliced

Directions:
1. Preheat oven to 350 degrees Fahrenheit.
2. In a small bowl, stir the Parmesan cheese into the ricotta cheese until well combined.
3. Heat a heavy stock pot over medium-high heat. When the pot is hot, add the ground beef and brown the meat, stirring to break it up as it browns. This should take about 10 minutes.
4. When the meat is browned, add the onions and sauté for 5-7 minutes more. Add the garlic and sauté for one more minute.
5. Carefully drain excess grease from the meat mixture. Stir the marinara sauce into the meat mixture and transfer half of it to a baking dish.
6. Lay a third of the mozzarella slices on top of the meat sauce in the dish, and then spread half the ricotta mixture on top of the mozzarella.
7. Repeat the process in a second layer, putting the rest of the meat sauce on top of the ricotta, followed by another third of the mozzarella slices and the other half of the ricotta mixture.
8. Finish the layering by putting the remaining mozzarella slices on top of everything in the dish.
9. Cover the dish with aluminum foil.
10. Place the covered baking dish on the oven's center rack
11. Bake until lasagna is bubbly, about 45 minutes.
12. Allow the lasagna to cool for a few minutes and then spoon into serving bowls.

Nutrition Information Per Serving:

- Total Fat: 25 grams
- Carbohydrates: 7 grams
- Protein: 25 grams

Keto Shepherd's Pie

Servings: 6
Time Required: About 45 minutes

Ingredients:
- 1 head cauliflower, core and leaves removed
- 4 Tbsp. butter
- 4 oz. cream cheese
- 1 egg
- 1 cup mozzarella cheese, grated
- Salt and pepper to taste
- 1 Tbsp. garlic powder
- 2 lbs. ground beef, 90 percent lean
- 2 cups carrots, sliced
- 2 cups frozen peas
- 8 oz. fresh white mushrooms, sliced
- 1 cup beef stock

Directions:
1. Using a steamer or a steamer pot on the stove top, steam the cauliflower until it's tender, about 15 minutes.
2. Transfer cauliflower to a blender or food processor. Add the butter, cream cheese, mozzarella, egg, and salt and pepper. Blend until the mixture is smooth.
3. In a medium bowl, mix together the ground beef, carrots, peas and mushrooms.
4. Place the meat and vegetable mixture into a stock pot, along with 1/2 cup water. Add the cauliflower mixture on top of the meat mixture.
5. Bring to a simmer. Cook until vegetables are tender, about 30 minutes. Add more water if necessary during the cooking process.
6. Spoon the hot shepherd's pie into serving bowls and serve immediately.

Nutrition Information Per Serving:
- Total Fat: 21 grams
- Carbohydrates: 4 grams
- Protein: 22 grams

Fish and Poultry

Fish, chicken and seafood are excellent sources of protein and healthy fatty acids, and every keto diet should include them. Use these recipes to get fish and seafood onto your weekly menu in the most delicious way possible.

Chicken Vindaloo

Servings: 6
Time Required: About 45 minutes

Ingredients:
- 1 lb. chicken thighs, boneless and skinless, cut into bite-size pieces
- 1 onion, diced
- 5 cloves garlic, minced
- 1 tsp. fresh ginger, peeled and minced
- 1 Tbsp. olive oil
- ¼ cup white vinegar
- 1 cup chopped tomato
- 1 tsp. salt
- 1 tsp. garam masala
- 1 tsp. smoked paprika
- ½ tsp. cayenne pepper
- ½ tsp. ground coriander
- ½ tsp. ground cumin
- ½ tsp. turmeric
- ¼ cup water

Directions:
1. Heat the oil in a heavy stock pot. Add the onions and sauté until they begin to brown, about 5 minutes. Add ginger and garlic and sauté for about a minute more.
2. Transfer the onions, garlic and ginger, along with cayenne, coriander, cumin, salt and pepper, to a blender or food processor. Blend to a smooth consistency.

3. Transfer the mixture to a medium mixing bowl and add the chicken, tossing to coat. Add ¼ cup water and turmeric and mix well. Cover the bowl and allow to marinate in the refrigerator for up to 8 hours.
4. After marinating, transfer the mixture back to the pot.
5. Bring to a simmer. Cook until the chicken is thoroughly cooked, about 30 minutes. Add more water if necessary during the cooking process.
6. If you'd like the sauce to be thicker, increase the heat and allow the sauce to reduce before serving.

Nutrition Information Per Serving:
- Total Fat: 8 grams
- Carbohydrates: 7 grams
- Protein: 23 grams

Chicken Tikka Masala

Servings: 6
Time Required: About 45 minutes

Ingredients:

- 1 ½ lb. chicken breast, boneless and skinless, cut into bite-size pieces
- ½ cup Greek-style yogurt
- 9 cloves garlic, minced
- 4 tsp. fresh ginger, peeled and minced
- 1 ½ tsp. turmeric
- ¾ tsp. cayenne pepper
- 1 ½ tsp. smoked paprika
- 2 tsp. salt
- 3 tsp. garam masala
- 1 ½ tsp. ground cumin
- 1 onion, chopped
- 14 oz. canned diced tomatoes
- 1 carrot, chopped
- 4 oz. half and half
- 1 tsp. garam masala
- ½ cup chopped cilantro

Directions:

1. In a medium bowl, mix together yogurt, 4 cloves garlic, 2 teaspoons ginger, ½ teaspoon turmeric, ¼ teaspoon cayenne, ½ teaspoon paprika, 1 teaspoon salt, 1 teaspoon garam masala and ½ teaspoon cumin.
2. Toss the chicken with this mixture and allow it to marinate for up to 2 hours.
3. Add onion, tomatoes, carrot, 5 cloves garlic, 2 teaspoons ginger, 1 teaspoon turmeric, ½ teaspoon cayenne, 1 teaspoon paprika, 1 teaspoon salt, 2 teaspoons garam masala and 1 teaspoon cumin to a stock pot.
4. Bring to a simmer. Cook until the chicken is thoroughly cooked, about 30 minutes. Add more water if necessary during the cooking process.
5. Remove the chicken from the sauce and set aside.
6. If you have an immersion blender, use it to puree the sauce in the pot. Otherwise, transfer the sauce to a blender or food processor and blend until smooth.
7. Stir in the half and half.
8. Return the chicken to the sauce and serve hot, garnished with cilantro.

Nutrition Information Per Serving:

- Total Fat: 6 grams
- Carbohydrates: 10 grams
- Protein: 18 grams

Creamy Ranch Chicken

Servings: 6
Time Required: About 45 minutes

Ingredients:
- 1 head cauliflower, chopped
- 1 lb. chicken breast, boneless and skinless, cut into cubes
- ½ cup prepared ranch dressing
- 4 oz. cream cheese
- 2 cups shredded cheddar cheese
- 2 cups chicken stock
- Salt and pepper to taste

Directions:
1. Add all the ingredients, excluding the cream cheese and cheddar cheese, to a large pot.
2. Bring to a simmer. Cook until the chicken is thoroughly cooked, about 30 minutes. Add more water if necessary during the cooking process.
3. Stir in the cream cheese and cheddar cheese, continuing to stir until the cheeses have melted.
4. Transfer to serving bowls and serve hot.

Nutrition Information Per Serving:
- Total Fat: 25 grams
- Carbohydrates: 8 grams
- Protein: 24 grams

Chicken Korma

Servings: 6
Time Required: About 45 minutes

Ingredients:
- 1 lb. chicken thighs, boneless and skinless, cut into bite-size pieces
- 1 oz. unsalted cashews
- 1 onion, chopped
- ½ cup tomatoes, diced
- ½ Serrano chili pepper, seeded and chopped
- 5 cloves garlic, minced
- 1 tsp. fresh ginger, peeled and minced
- 1 tsp. turmeric
- 1 tsp. salt
- 1 tsp. garam masala
- ½ tsp. cumin
- ½ tsp. coriander
- ½ tsp. cayenne pepper
- ½ cup water
- ½ cup unsweetened coconut milk

Directions:
1. In a blender or food processor, combine cashews, onion, tomatoes, chili pepper, ginger, garlic, turmeric, salt, garam masala, cumin, coriander and cayenne. Blend until the mixture is smooth.
2. Pour the blended mixture into a large pot. Use ½ cup water to rinse the blender jar, and pour the water into the pot.
3. Stir the chicken into the mixture in the pot.
4. Bring to a simmer. Cook until the chicken is thoroughly cooked, about 30 minutes. Add more water if necessary during the cooking process.
5. Stir in the coconut milk and serve the mixture hot, garnished with chopped fresh cilantro.

Nutrition Information Per Serving:
- Total Fat: 19 grams
- Carbohydrates: 6 grams
- Protein: 14 grams

Spicy Shredded Chicken

Servings: 6
Time Required: About 45 minutes

Ingredients:

- 1 ½ lbs. chicken thighs, boneless and skinless
- 1 Tbsp. olive oil
- 2 tomatillos, thinly sliced
- ½ onion, thinly sliced
- 4 cloves garlic, minced
- 1/3 cup chicken stock
- 7 oz. canned roasted tomatoes
- 1 Tbsp. adobo chipotle chili, chopped
- ½ tsp. ground cumin
- ¼ tsp. ground cinnamon
- ½ tsp. dried oregano
- 1 Tbsp. soy sauce
- 1 Tbsp. cider vinegar

Directions:

1. Heat the oil in a large, heavy pot. When the oil is hot, add the tomatillos and onions. Sauté until the vegetables are browned, about 7-10 minutes.
2. Add the garlic and sauté a minute more.
3. Add chicken stock and tomatoes, stirring to deglaze the pot liner.
4. Add the chipotle chili, cumin, cinnamon, oregano, soy sauce, and vinegar. Sauté until fragrant, about another minute.
5. Add the chicken and stop the Sauté cycle.
6. Bring to a simmer. Cook until the chicken is thoroughly cooked, about 30 minutes. Add more water if necessary during the cooking process.
7. Remove the chicken and transfer to a plate. Allow it to cool slightly and then shred it with a fork or your fingers.
8. Using an immersion blender, blend the sauce until it's a smooth puree.
9. Return the chicken to pot. Allow the pot to reheat until the mixture is heated through and the sauce has thickened a bit.
10. Serve the chicken with its sauce over riced cauliflower.

Nutrition Information Per Serving:

- Total Fat: 7 grams
- Carbohydrates: 4 grams
- Protein: 25 grams

Butter Chicken

Servings: 6
Time Required: About 45 minutes

Ingredients:
- 2 lbs. chicken thighs, boneless and skinless, cut into large pieces
- 14 oz. canned diced tomatoes
- 6 cloves garlic, minced
- 2 tsp. fresh ginger, peeled and minced
- 1 tsp. turmeric
- ½ tsp. cayenne pepper
- 1 tsp. paprika
- 1 tsp. salt
- 1 tsp. garam masala
- 1 tsp. ground cumin
- 1 cup chicken stock
- 4 oz. butter, cubed
- 4 oz. heavy cream

Directions:
1. Put tomatoes, garlic, ginger, turmeric, cayenne, paprika, salt, garam masala, and cumin in a large pot. Mix well.
2. Add the chicken to the pot, tossing to coat it with the sauce ingredients.
3. Add the chicken stock to the pot.
4. Transfer the chicken to a plate and set aside.
5. Using an immersion blender, blend the sauce until it's smooth.
6. Add the butter and cream, stirring until the butter is melted.
7. Return the chicken to the pot and mix well.
8. Transfer to a serving platter and serve hot, garnished with chopped fresh cilantro.

Nutrition Information Per Serving:
- Total Fat: 20 grams
- Carbohydrates: 3 grams
- Protein: 25 grams

Garlic Chicken

Servings: 4-6
Time Required: About 45 minutes

Ingredients:

- 1 lb. chicken thighs, boneless and skinless
- 2 tsp. Herbs de Provence
- 1 Tbsp. olive oil
- 1 Tbsp. Dijon mustard
- 1 Tbsp. cider vinegar
- 1 tsp. salt
- 1 tsp. freshly ground black pepper
- 2 cloves garlic, minced
- 2 Tbsp. butter
- 8 cloves garlic, sliced
- ¼ cup water
- ¼ cup heavy cream

Directions:

1. In a medium bowl, mix together herbs, olive oil, mustard, vinegar, minced garlic, salt and pepper. Toss the chicken in the mixture to coat. Cover with plastic wrap and allow to marinate at room temperature for 30 minutes.
2. Heat the butter in a large pot over medium-high heat. When the butter has melted, add the sliced garlic and sauté just until the garlic is fragrant, about a minute.
3. Add the chicken to the pot, reserving the marinade in the bowl. Sauté the chicken to brown it on both sides, turning it halfway through. This should take about 2 minutes per side.
4. Add the marinade to the pot, along with about ¼ cup water.
5. Cover the pot and continue to sauté for about 10 minutes, turning the chicken once during the process. Your goal is to get the chicken to an internal temperature of 165 degrees Fahrenheit; you can use a meat thermometer to check.
6. When the chicken has reached the correct temperature, transfer it to a serving platter.
7. Stir the cream into the pot and heat the sauce thoroughly.
8. When the sauce has thickened slightly, pour it over the chicken and serve immediately.

Nutrition Information Per Serving:

- Total Fat: 37 grams
- Carbohydrates: 4 grams
- Protein: 19 grams

Mexican-Style Chicken

Servings: 6
Time Required: About 40 minutes

Ingredients:
- 2 lbs. boneless skinless chicken thighs boneless, chopped
- 1 Tbsp. ground cumin
- 1 Tbsp. chili powder
- 1 Tbsp. salt
- 2 Tbsp. olive oil
- 14 oz. canned diced tomatoes
- 5 oz. tomato paste
- 1 onion, chopped
- 3 cloves garlic, minced
- 1 cup chicken stock

Directions:
1. In a medium bowl, combine cumin, chili powder and salt. Toss the chicken in the spice mixture to coat.
2. Heat the oil in a heavy pot over medium-high heat. When the oil is hot, sauté the chicken for about 5 minutes.
3. Add all the other ingredients to the pot.
4. Bring to a simmer. Cook until the chicken is thoroughly cooked, about 20 minutes. Add more water if necessary during the cooking process.
5. Transfer for to a serving platter and serve hot.

Nutrition Information Per Serving:
- Total Fat: 22 grams
- Carbohydrates: 4 grams
- Protein: 19 grams

Neapolitan Chicken

Servings: 6
Time Required: About 35 minutes

Ingredients:
- 6 chicken thighs, with skin
- 2 Tbsp. olive oil
- 2 cloves garlic, crushed
- Salt and pepper
- ½ tsp. red chili flakes
- 14 oz. canned chopped tomatoes
- ½ cup black olives, pitted
- 1 Tbsp. capers
- 1 Tbsp. fresh basil, chopped
- ¾ cup water

Directions:
1. Heat oil for a minute in a large, heavy pot and then place chicken carefully in the pot, skin side down. Brown chicken without turning for about 5 minutes. When chicken is browned, remove from the pot and set aside.
2. Add tomatoes, olives, garlic, capers, basil, chili flakes and water to the pot. Season with salt and pepper to taste. Stir to combine and heat to a simmer.
3. When the mixture begins to simmer, add the chicken to the pot.
4. Return to a simmer. Cook until the chicken is thoroughly cooked, about 20 minutes. Add more water if necessary during the cooking process.

Nutrition Information Per Serving:
- Total Fat: 20 grams
- Carbohydrates: 10 grams
- Protein: 38 grams

Italian Chicken

Servings: 4
Time Required: About 40 minutes

Ingredients:
- 4 chicken thighs, with the bone, skinless
- Salt and pepper to taste
- Olive oil spray
- 14 oz. crushed tomatoes
- ½ onion, diced
- 1 bell pepper, diced
- ½ tsp. oregano

Directions:
1. Season chicken with salt and pepper, flipping to season both sides equally.
2. Spray a heavy pot with a light coating of oil. Brown the chicken in the pot, turning to brown all sides, then remove from the pot and put aside.
3. Spray the pot with oil again, and then sauté onions and peppers until soft and beginning to brown, approximately 5 minutes.
4. Put the chicken back into the pot. Add tomatoes, oregano, bay leaf, salt and pepper. Stir and cover.
5. Simmer until chicken is thoroughly cooked, about 25 minutes.

Nutrition Information Per Serving:
- Total Fat: 3 grams
- Carbohydrates: 10.5 grams
- Protein: 14 grams

Lemon Chicken

Servings: 6
Time Required: About 30 minutes

Ingredients:
- 2 lbs. chicken breasts or thighs
- 1 tsp. kosher salt
- 1 onion, chopped
- 1 Tbsp. olive oil
- 5 cloves garlic, minced
- ½ cup chicken stock

Directions:
1. Heat oil in a heavy-bottomed pot. When the oil is heated, after about a minute, add the onion. Sauté, stirring, until the onion is soft and translucent.
2. Add the chicken, stock, salt, and garlic.
3. Cover and simmer until chicken is cooked, about 25-30 minutes.
4. Remove the lid and serve chicken with sauce from the pot.
5. Serves four.

Nutrition Information Per Serving:
- Total Fat: 25 grams
- Carbohydrates: 9 grams
- Protein: 27 grams

Cheesy Bacon Chicken

Servings: 6
Time Required: About 35 minutes

Ingredients:
- 8 slices bacon, cooked crisp and crumbled
- 2 lbs. chicken breast, boneless and skinless, cut into large pieces
- 1 packet ranch dressing mix
- 8 oz. cream cheese
- ½ cup water
- 1 cup cheddar cheese, grated

Directions:
1. Place the chicken, cream cheese and water into a large pot.
2. Sprinkle the ranch dressing mix over the top of the chicken and cream cheese.
3. Cover and simmer until the chicken is cooked, about 25-30 minutes.
4. Stir in the bacon and cheddar cheese, continuing to stir as the mixture reheats until the cheese is melted.
5. Transfer to serving bowls. Serve hot.

Nutrition Information Per Serving:
- Total Fat: 34 grams
- Carbohydrates: 2 grams
- Protein: 58 grams

One-Pot Curry-Style Chicken

Servings: 3
Time Required: About 35 minutes

Ingredients:
- 3 chicken breast fillets, boneless and skinless
- ½ onion, chopped
- ½ tsp. ground ginger
- 4 cloves garlic, minced
- 2 tsp. curry powder
- 2 tsp. ground cumin
- 1 Tbsp. cider vinegar
- 1 Tbsp. fresh lemon juice
- 1 cup chicken stock

Directions:
1. Put all the ingredients in a large pot.
2. Cover and simmer until the chicken is done and the spices are fragrant, about 30 minutes.
3. Remove the chicken and shred, then return it to the pot to reheat in the sauce.
4. Serve over roasted cauliflower. Serves three.

Nutrition Information Per Serving:
- Total Fat: 9 grams
- Carbohydrates: 3 grams
- Protein: 22 grams

Spicy Braised Cod

Servings: 3
Time Required: About 25 minutes

Ingredients:
- 1 lb. cod filets
- 1 onion, chopped
- 1 bell pepper, chopped
- 1 jalapeno pepper, seeded and chopped
- 2 small tomatoes, chopped
- 2 cloves garlic, minced
- 2 cups chicken stock
- 1 tsp. kosher salt
- ¼ tsp. black pepper
- 1 Tbsp. olive oil

Directions:
1. Heat the oil in a large, heavy skillet. When the oil is hot, add the onions, jalapeno, and bell pepper and sauté until soft. Add the garlic and sauté 1 minute more.
2. Add the rest of the ingredients.
3. Bring to simmer and cook just until the cod is done, about 15 minutes.
4. Serve the fish and sauce over cauliflower.

Nutrition Information Per Serving:
- Total Fat: 5 grams
- Carbohydrates: 9.5 grams
- Protein: 11 grams

Keto Jambalaya

Servings: 6-8
Time Required: About 40 minutes

Ingredients:
- 1 lb. cooked, peeled shrimp
- 1 lb. cooked chicken breast, cubed
- 1 lb. andouille sausage, sliced
- ½ cup chicken stock
- ½ onion, diced
- 1 bell pepper, diced
- 14 oz. crushed tomato
- 2 cloves garlic, minced
- 1 Tbsp. olive oil
- 1 Tbsp. Cajun seasoning
- ½ tsp. hot sauce

Directions:
1. Heat the oil over medium-high heat in a large pot. When the oil is hot, add the onion and bell pepper and sauté until soft. Add the garlic and sauté 1 minute more.
2. Add the sausage to the pot and sauté, stirring, until the sausage is brown.
3. Add the rest of the ingredients, then cover the pot.
4. Bring to a simmer and cook until the vegetables are tender, about 30 minutes.
5. Serve the jambalaya over steamed cauliflower.

Nutrition Information Per Serving:
- Total Fat: 9 grams
- Carbohydrates: 15 grams
- Protein: 32 grams

Easy Shrimp

Servings: 6
Time Required: About 10 minutes

Ingredients:
- 2 lbs. shrimp, peeled and cooked
- 2 Tbsp. olive oil
- 2 Tbsp. butter
- 2 cloves garlic, minced
- ½ cup white wine
- ½ cup chicken stock

Directions:
1. Heat the oil in a large skillet over medium-high heat. Add the garlic and sauté 1 minute.
2. Add the rest of the ingredients.
3. Allow to simmer just until the shrimp are heated through, about 4 minutes
4. Serve the shrimp over steamed cauliflower.

Nutrition Information Per Serving:
- Total Fat: 4 grams
- Carbohydrates: 1 gram
- Protein: 21 grams

Pressure Cooker Whole Lobster

Servings: 2
Time Required: About 10 minutes

Ingredients:
- 2-lbs. live lobster
- 1 cup white wine
- 3 cups water

Directions:
1. Add the water and wine to the pot.
2. Put the live lobster in an electronic pressure cooker, then cover and lock the pot.
3. Set the cook time for 3 minutes at high pressure.
4. At the end of the cook time, carefully vent the pot manually.
5. Allow the lobster to cool slightly before serving.

Nutrition Information Per Serving:
- Total Fat: 1 gram
- Carbohydrates: 2 grams
- Protein: 36 grams

Pressure Cooker Crab Legs

Servings: 4
Time Required: About 10 minutes

Ingredients:
- 2 lbs. frozen crab legs
- ¾ cups water
- Butter
- Fresh lemons, quartered

Directions:
1. Place steamer basket in the pot.
2. Add the water to the pot.
3. Put the crab legs into the pot, then cover and lock the pot.
4. Set the cook time for 2 minutes at high pressure.
5. At the end of the cook time, carefully vent the pot manually.
6. Serve the crab legs hot with melted butter and lemon quarters.

Nutrition Information Per Serving (excluding butter):
- Total Fat: 1 gram
- Carbohydrates: 0 gram
- Protein: 38 grams

Teriyaki Scallops

Servings: 4
Time Required: About 10 minutes

Ingredients:
- 1 Tbsp. olive oil
- 1 lb. fresh sea scallops
- ½ cup coconut-based soy-style sauce
- 3 Tbsp. 100% maple syrup
- ½ tsp. garlic powder
- ½ tsp. ground ginger
- ½ tsp. kosher salt

Directions:
1. Heat oil in a large, heavy skillet over medium-high heat.
2. When the oil is hot, add the scallops and sear, turning so that they brown on both sides, about one minute per side.
3. Stir together the rest of the ingredients and then pour over the scallops in the skillet.
4. Sautee just until scallops are heated through, about 2 minutes.
5. Serve the scallops drizzled with sauce from the pot.

Nutrition Information Per Serving:
- Total Fat: 6 grams
- Carbohydrates: 26 grams
- Protein: 25 grams

Fish Curry

Servings: 4
Time Required: About 20 minutes

Ingredients:
- 1 lb. firm fish such as halibut or cod
- 1 onion, chopped
- 3 cloves garlic, minced
- 2 Tbsp. fresh ginger, peeled and minced
- 1 tomato, chopped
- ¼ cup unsweetened coconut, shredded
- 3 tsp. olive oil
- 2 tsp. turmeric
- ¼ tsp. dry mustard
- ¼ tsp. cumin
- ¼ tsp. cayenne pepper
- 1 tsp. garam masala
- 1 cup water
- Salt to taste

Directions:
1. Heat the oil in a large pot over medium-high heat. When the oil is hot, add the onions to the pot and sauté until soft and translucent, about 5 minutes.
2. Add garlic to the pot and sauté for one minute more.
3. Stir in tomato, spices, coconut and water. Cook until the sauce has thickened, about 5 minutes.
4. Add the fish to the pot and stir to combine.
5. Simmer just until the fish is firm and thoroughly cooked, about 10-15 minutes.
6. Serve the fish and sauce over cauliflower.

Nutrition Information Per Serving:
- Total Fat: 8 grams
- Carbohydrates: 7 grams
- Protein: 24 grams

Crab Egg Bake

Servings: 4
Time Required: About 40 minutes

Ingredients:
- 4 eggs, beaten
- 8 oz. lump crab meat or imitation crab
- 1 cup half and half
- ½ tsp. salt
- 1 tsp. freshly ground pepper
- 1 tsp. smoked paprika
- ½ tsp. dried thyme
- 1 cup Swiss cheese, grated
- 1 cup spring onions, chopped

Directions:
1. Preheat oven to 350 degrees Fahrenheit.
2. In a mixing bowl, whisk together eggs and half and half.
3. Whisk in salt, pepper, thyme, and paprika.
4. Stir in cheese and spring onions.
5. Stir in crab meat.
6. Pour mixture into a baking dish. Cover the dish with foil and place on oven's center rack.
7. Bake until egg is set, about 25-30 minutes.
8. Serve the crab bake hot or allow to cool to room temperature.

Nutrition Information Per Serving:
- Total Fat: 25 grams
- Carbohydrates: 19 grams
- Protein: 22 grams

Asian-Style Salmon

Servings: 4
Time Required: About 60 minutes

Ingredients:
- 1 lb. salmon filets
- 1 Tbsp. soy sauce
- 2 tsp. fresh ginger, peeled and minced
- 1 clove garlic, minced
- ½ tsp. salt
- 1 tsp. freshly ground black pepper

Directions:
1. Preheat oven to 350 degrees Fahrenheit.
2. In a small bowl, mix soy sauce, garlic, ginger, salt and pepper.
3. Place salmon in a shallow baking dish.
4. Pour seasoning mixture over the salmon. Allow the fish to marinate for 30 minutes.
5. Place the dish on the oven's center rack.
6. Bake until salmon is flaky but not dry, about 20-25 minutes.
7. Transfer the salmon to serving plates and serve hot.

Nutrition Information Per Serving:
- Total Fat: 7 grams
- Carbohydrates: 0 gram
- Protein: 23 grams

Coconut Shrimp

Servings: 4
Time Required: About 10 minutes

Ingredients:
- 1 lb. shrimp, peeled and uncooked
- 1 Tbsp. fresh ginger, peeled and minced
- 3 cloves garlic, minced
- ½ tsp. turmeric
- 1 tsp. salt
- ½ tsp. cayenne pepper
- 1 tsp. garam masala
- 8 oz. unsweetened coconut milk

Directions:
1. Preheat oven to 400 degrees Fahrenheit.
2. In a mixing bowl, combine all ingredients, tossing in shrimp to thoroughly coat them with the seasoning mixture.
3. Transfer mixture to a baking dish.
4. Place the baking dish on the oven's center rack.
5. Roast just until shrimp are firm and opaque, about 6-8 minutes.
6. Serve hot.

Nutrition Information Per Serving:
- Total Fat: 12 grams
- Carbohydrates: 4 grams
- Protein: 16 grams

Greek-Style Shrimp

Servings: 4
Time Required: About 15 minutes

Ingredients:
- 1 lb. shrimp, peeled
- 2 Tbsp. butter
- 3 cloves garlic, minced
- ½ tsp. red pepper flakes
- 1 onion, chopped
- 14 oz. canned diced tomatoes
- 1 tsp. dried oregano
- 1 tsp. salt
- 1 cup feta cheese, crumbled
- ½ cup black olives, sliced
- ¼ cup fresh parsley, chopped

Directions:
1. Heat the butter in a large pot over medium-high heat. Once the butter has melted, add the onion and pepper flakes and sauté until the onion is translucent, about 5 minutes. Add the garlic and sauté for about a minute more.
2. Add the tomatoes, oregano, salt and shrimp.
3. Simmer just until shrimp is opaque and cooked through, about 5 minutes.
4. Transfer to a serving platter and top with feta, olives and parsley.
5. Serve with riced cauliflower.

Nutrition Information Per Serving:
- Total Fat: 11 grams
- Carbohydrates: 6 grams
- Protein: 19 grams

Ginger Fish

Servings: 4
Time Required: About 1 hour

Ingredients:
- 1 lb. firm fish, such as tilapia or flounder
- 3 Tbsp. soy sauce
- 2 Tbsp. rice wine
- 1 Tbsp. black bean paste
- 1 tsp. fresh ginger, peeled and minced
- 1 clove garlic, minced

Directions:
1. Preheat oven to 350 degrees Fahrenheit.
2. In a small bowl, mix together soy sauce, rice wine, bean paste, ginger and garlic. Season with salt and pepper.
3. Pour the seasoning mixture over the fish in a shallow baking dish and allow to marinate for 30 minutes.
4. Place the baking dish on the oven's center rack and bake until fish is firm and flaky, about 15-20 minutes.
5. Serve the fish hot, garnished with chopped spring onions.

Nutrition Information Per Serving:
- Total Fat: 3 grams
- Carbohydrates: 4 grams
- Protein: 24 grams

Veggies and Side Dishes

Meat, poultry and fish are a big part of most keto diets, but it's possible to prepare vegetarian dishes that fit well within the requirements of a keto-friendly nutrition plan. The recipes in this section include main dishes, vegetable side dishes and desserts, all of them vegetarian and some them vegan-friendly, as well. Be sure, also, to check the Soups and Stews and Side Dishes sections for more vegetarian and vegan recipes.

Palak Paneer

Servings: 4
Time Required: About 10 minutes

Ingredients:
- 1 lb. fresh spinach
- 1 ½ cups paneer
- 2 tsp. olive oil
- 5 cloves garlic, minced
- 1 Tbsp. fresh ginger, peeled and minced
- 1 onion, chopped
- 2 tomatoes, chopped
- 2 tsp. ground cumin
- ½ tsp. cayenne pepper
- 2 tsp. garam masala
- 1 tsp. turmeric
- 1 tsp. salt
- ½ cup water

Directions:
1. Heat the oil in a large, heavy skillet over medium-high heat. When the oil is hot, add the garlic and ginger and sauté just until fragrant, about 30 seconds.
2. Add the rest of the ingredients, excluding the paneer, and stir to combine.
3. Sautee until the spinach is wilted and the spices are fragrant, about 4-5 minutes.
4. Carefully add the paneer to the pot, stirring gently to combine.
5. Serve hot.

Nutrition Information Per Serving:

- Total Fat: 16 grams
- Carbohydrates: 8 grams
- Protein: 11 grams

Pressure Cooker Keto Cake

Servings: 4
Time Required: About 75 minutes

Ingredients:
- 1 cup almond flour
- ½ cup unsweetened coconut, shredded
- 1/3 cup Stevia sweetener
- 1 tsp. baking powder
- ½ tsp. cinnamon
- 2 eggs, lightly beaten
- ¼ cup butter, melted
- ½ cup heavy whipping cream

Directions:
1. In a medium bowl, combine almond flour, coconut, sweetener, baking powder and cinnamon.
2. Whisk in eggs, butter and cream, one at a time, until all ingredients are well combined.
3. Pour the mixture into a pan that's small enough to fit into your electronic pressure cooker. Cover the pan with foil.
4. Place the steamer rack into the pressure cooker and pour in 2 cups of water.
5. Place the pan onto the steamer rack.
6. Cover and lock the pot.
7. Set the cook time for 40 minutes.
8. At the end of the cook time, allow the pot to vent naturally for 10 minutes.
9. After 10 minutes, carefully release any remaining steam and uncover the pot.
10. Remove the pan from the pot and allow to cool for 15 minutes. After the cake has cooled, flip the pan over and carefully encourage the cake out of the pan.

Nutrition Information Per Serving:
- Total Fat: 23 grams
- Carbohydrates: 5 grams
- Protein: 5 grams

Spicy Mushrooms

Servings: 2
Time Required: About 20 minutes

Ingredients:
- 8 oz. white mushrooms, chopped
- 2 large chili peppers, such as guajillo, poblano or New Mexico, seeded and chopped
- 1 tsp. olive oil
- 1 onion, chopped
- 6 cloves garlic, minced
- 1 tsp. ground cumin
- ½ tsp. dried oregano
- ½ tsp. smoked paprika
- ¼ tsp. ground cinnamon
- ¼ tsp. salt
- ¼ cup water
- 1 tsp. cider vinegar

Directions:
1. Heat the oil in a large skillet over medium-high heat. When the oil is hot, add the onions to the pan and sauté until soft and translucent, about 5 minutes.
2. Add garlic to the pan and sauté for one minute more.
3. Transfer half of the onion and garlic to a blender or food processor.
4. Add mushrooms to the skillet and cook for 5 minutes more.
5. Meanwhile, add chilis to the blender or food processor. Add cumin, oregano, paprika, cinnamon, salt and water. Blend until smooth.
6. Transfer the blended sauce mixture to the skillet.
7. Simmer until the sauce is heated through and bubbly, about 5 minutes.
8. Serve the mushrooms hot with steamed cauliflower.

Nutrition Information Per Serving:
- Total Fat: 12 grams
- Carbohydrates: 16 grams
- Protein: 4 grams

Cauliflower Curry

Servings: 4-6
Time Required: About 30 minutes

Ingredients:
- 1 head cauliflower, chopped
- ½ onion, chopped
- 2 tomatoes, chopped
- 6 cloves garlic, minced
- 1 Tbsp. fresh ginger, peeled and minced
- ½ jalapeno chili, diced
- 1 tsp. olive oil
- ½ tsp. turmeric
- 1 tsp. ground cumin
- ½ tsp. garam masala
- ¾ tsp. salt
- ½ tsp. paprika

Directions:
1. Place onion, tomato, chili, ginger and garlic in a blender or food processor and blend until smooth.
2. Heat the oil in a large skillet over medium-high heat. When the oil is hot, add mixture from the blender to the pan.
3. Add the spices to the pan and stir to mix. Simmer for 5 minutes.
4. Stir the cauliflower into the pan and simmer until tender, about 15 minutes.
5. Serve hot.

Nutrition Information Per Serving:
- Total Fat: 1 gram
- Carbohydrates: 20 grams
- Protein: 4 grams

Pressure Cooker Carrot Cake

Servings: 4-6
Time Required: About 70 minutes

Ingredients:
- 3 eggs
- 1 cup almond flour
- 2/3 cup Stevia-based sweetener
- 1 tsp. baking powder
- ½ Tbsp. apple pie spice
- ¼ cup coconut oil
- ½ cup heavy cream
- 1 cup carrots, shredded
- ½ cup walnuts, chopped

Directions:
1. In a medium mixing bowl, mix all the ingredients using an electric mixer until the batter is well-mixed and fluffy.
2. Pour batter into a greased cake pan that's small enough to fit into your electronic pressure cooker. Cover the pan with aluminum foil.
3. Place the steamer rack in the cooker and pour in 2 cups of water.
4. Place the pan on the steamer rack.
5. Cover and lock the pot.
6. Cook at high pressure for 40 minutes.
7. At the end of the cooking cycle, allow the pot to vent naturally for 10 minutes. After 10 minutes, carefully vent any remaining pressure and uncover the pot.
8. Remove the pan from the pot and allow the cake to cool before serving.

Nutrition Information Per Serving:
- Total Fat: 25 grams
- Carbohydrates: 6 grams
- Protein: 6 grams

Green Chili Cheese Bake

Servings: 4
Time Required: About 35 minutes

Ingredients:
- 4 eggs, beaten
- 1 cup half and half
- 10 oz. canned green chilis
- ½ tsp. salt
- ½ tsp. ground cumin
- 1 cup Monterey Jack cheese, grated
- ¼ cup fresh cilantro, chopped

Directions:
1. Preheat oven to 350 degrees Fahrenheit.
2. In a medium bowl, combine eggs, half and half, chilis, cheese, salt and cumin.
3. Pour the mixture into a greased baking pan. Cover the pan with aluminum foil.
4. Place the pan on the oven's center rack and bake until the egg is set, about 25-30 minutes.
5. Remove the pan from the pot and allow to cool slightly before serving.

Nutrition Information Per Serving:
- Total Fat: 19 grams
- Carbohydrates: 6 grams
- Protein: 14 grams

Indian-Style Eggplant

Servings: 4
Time Required: About 30 minutes

Ingredients:
- 1 medium eggplant, peeled and sliced
- 1/3 cup olive oil
- 3 cloves garlic, minced
- ½ onion, chopped
- ¼ tsp. turmeric
- 1/8 tsp. cayenne pepper
- ½ tsp. salt
- 1/3 cup tomatoes, diced
- ½ cup water
- 2 Tbsp. fresh cilantro, chopped

Directions:
1. Heat 2 tablespoons of the olive oil in a large, heavy skillet. Once the oil is hot, add enough eggplant slices to cover the bottom of the pot liner. Allow the eggplant to brown well on the bottom, and add more eggplant as the slices shrink. Add more oil as necessary.
2. When the eggplant is browned and softened, add the onions and sauté for 5 minutes more.
3. Add the garlic and sauté for another minute.
4. Add the turmeric, cayenne, and salt. Sauté until fragrant, about a minute.
5. Add the tomatoes and water, and stir to combine everything in the pan.
6. Bring to a simmer and cook until the eggplant is fully cooked, about 15 minutes.
7. Transfer the eggplant and sauce to a serving platter.
8. Serve hot, garnished with cilantro.

Nutrition Information Per Serving:
- Total Fat: 12 grams
- Carbohydrates: 6 grams
- Protein: 1 gram

Spaghetti Squash

Servings: 4
Time Required: About 60 minutes

Ingredients:
- 1 spaghetti squash, medium

Directions:
1. Preheat oven to 400 degrees Fahrenheit.
2. With a sharp knife, carefully cut the squash in half crosswise, across the short length of the squash instead of along the longer axis.
3. Place the squash halves on a baking sheet, cut side down.
4. Place the baking sheet on the oven's center rack and roast until the squash is tender, about 45-50 minutes.
5. Remove the squash and, while it's still hot, carefully shred the flesh into spaghetti-like strands with a fork.
6. Serve the squash hot with butter.

Nutrition Information Per Serving:
- Total Fat: 1 gram
- Carbohydrates: 7 grams
- Protein: 1 gram

Steamed Artichokes

Servings: 4
Time Required: About 40 minutes

Ingredients:
- 4 artichokes, medium-sized
- 1 lemon
- 4 cups vegetable stock
- ¼ tsp. kosher salt

Directions:
1. Trim the artichoke stems to an inch in length. Trim the other end of the artichokes, too, cutting the inch from the ends of the leaves. Discard the trimmings.
2. Slice the lemon into four slices.
3. Place the steamer rack into the steamer pot and place the lemon slices on the rack. Place the artichokes, stem end up, on the lemon slices, one artichoke on each lemon slice.
4. Pour the stock carefully into the pot. Season with salt.
5. Cover the pot.
6. Steam until the artichokes are tender, about 25-35 minutes.
7. Serve the artichokes with melted butter for dipping.

Nutrition Information Per Serving:
- Total Fat: 1 gram
- Carbohydrates: 13 grams
- Protein: 4 grams

Cheesy Cauliflower Casserole

Servings: 4-6
Time Required: About 60 minutes

Ingredients:
- 1 head cauliflower
- 2 eggs
- 2 Tbsp. heavy cream
- 2 oz. cream cheese
- ½ cup sour cream
- ½ cup parmesan cheese, grated
- 1 cup cheddar cheese, grated
- 2 Tbsp. butter
- 1 cup water

Directions:
1. Preheat oven to 350 degrees Fahrenheit.
2. Add eggs, cream, sour cream, cream cheese, parmesan and cheddar cheese to a blender or food processor. Blend to combine.
3. Add cauliflower to the food processor and blend, pulsing so that you can stop when the mixture is still chunky, not smooth.
4. Grease a casserole pan and pour the mixture into the pan.
5. Place the pan on the oven's center rack and bake until the casserole is bubbly, about 45 minutes.
6. Remove the pan and serve the casserole hot.

Nutrition Information Per Serving:
- Total Fat: 28 grams
- Carbohydrates: 7 grams
- Protein: 17 grams

Mashed Cauliflower

Servings: 4-6
Time Required: About 20 minutes

Ingredients:
- 1 head cauliflower
- 1/8 tsp. salt
- 1/8 tsp. freshly ground black pepper
- ¼ tsp. garlic powder
- 1 cup water

Directions:
1. Chop the cauliflower coarsely and discard the tough core.
2. Place a steamer rack in a steamer pot and add a cup of water.
3. Place the cauliflower on top of the steamer rack.
4. Steam until the cauliflower is tender, about 15 minutes.
5. Carefully drain the water and remove the steamer rack, returning the cauliflower to the pot once it's drained.
6. If you have an immersion blender, use it to blend the cauliflower to a smooth puree, adding the seasonings as you blend. If you don't have an immersion blender, transfer the cauliflower to a blender or food processor. Optionally, you can add a tablespoon of butter as you blend for a creamier consistency.
7. Serve hot.

Nutrition Information Per Serving:
- Total Fat: 1 gram
- Carbohydrates: 5 grams
- Protein: 2 grams

Braised Brussels Sprouts

Servings: 4-6
Time Required: About 25 minutes

Ingredients:
- 4 cups brussels sprouts, ends trimmed and cut in half
- 1 tsp. olive oil
- ½ cup water
- Salt to taste

Directions:
1. Heat the oil over medium-high heat in a heavy skillet. When the oil is hot, sauté the brussels sprouts, stirring frequently, until the sprouts are beginning to brown and get crisp at the edges. This should take about 5 minutes.
2. When the sprouts are browned, carefully add the water to the pot.
3. Cover and simmer until the sprouts are tender, about 15 minutes.
4. Remove the cover and season the brussels sprout with sea salt to taste.
5. Serve hot.

Nutrition Information Per Serving:
- Total Fat: 1 gram
- Carbohydrates: 8 grams
- Protein: 3 grams

Keema Curry

Servings: 4-6
Time Required: About 30 minutes

Ingredients:
- 2 Tbsp. olive oil
- 1 onion, diced
- 4 cloves garlic, minced
- 1 inch piece of fresh ginger, peeled and minced
- 1 Serrano pepper, seeded and minced
- 1 Tbsp. coriander
- 1 tsp. paprika
- 1 tsp. salt
- ½ tsp. turmeric
- ½ tsp. black pepper
- ½ tsp. garam masala
- ½ tsp. cumin powder
- ¼ tsp. cayenne
- ¼ tsp. ground cardamom
- 1 lb. ground beef
- 1 can diced tomatoes
- 2 cups fresh or frozen peas

Directions:
1. Heat the oil over medium-high heat in a large skillet. When the oil is hot, sauté the onions until they are beginning to brown, about 8 minutes.
2. Add garlic, ginger, Serrano pepper, and spices, and sauté for about 1 minute more.
3. Add the ground beef and sauté until the meat is thoroughly browned, about 5-10 minutes.
4. Add the tomatoes and peas to the pan, stirring to combine all the ingredients.
5. Simmer until the spices are fragrant and the sauce is bubbly, about 15 minutes.
6. Serve the curry hot.

Nutrition Information Per Serving:
- Total Fat: 20 grams
- Carbohydrates: 17 grams
- Protein: 30 grams

Coconut Cabbage

Servings: 4-6
Time Required: About 25 minutes

Ingredients:
- 1 Tbsp. olive oil
- 1 medium onion, sliced
- 1 tsp. salt
- 2 cloves garlic, minced
- ½ Thai red chili, seeded and sliced
- 1 tsp. dry mustard
- 1 Tbsp. curry powder
- 1 Tbsp. turmeric powder
- 1 Asian cabbage, cored and shredded
- 1 carrot, peeled and sliced
- 2 lemon juice
- ½ cup dried unsweetened coconut, shredded
- 1/3 cup water

Directions:
1. Heat the oil in a large skillet over medium-high heat. When the oil is hot, sauté the onions until they are soft and translucent, about 5 minutes.
2. Add garlic, chili pepper and spices and sauté for about 30 seconds more, just until fragrant.
3. Add the cabbage, carrot, lemon juice and water, stirring to combine.
4. Simmer until the vegetable are tender, about 15 minutes.
5. Remove the cover and serve the cabbage hot as a side dish.

Nutrition Information Per Serving:
- Total Fat: 1 gram
- Carbohydrates: 6 grams
- Protein: 1 gram

Garlic Zucchini

Servings: 4
Time Required: About 10 minutes

Ingredients:
- 2 large zucchini, peeled and coarsely grated
- 2 Tbsp. olive oil
- 2 cloves garlic, minced
- 1 tsp. lemon zest
- ½ tsp. sea salt
- 1 Tbsp. fresh lemon juice
- Salt and pepper to taste

Directions:
1. Heat the oil in a large skillet over medium-high heat. When the oil is hot, sauté the garlic and lemon zest just until fragrant, about 30 seconds.
2. Add the zucchini and season to taste with salt and pepper. Sprinkle lemon juice over the top of the zucchini.
3. Sauté, stirring, just until zucchini is heated through, about 2 or 3 minutes.
4. Remove from the pot and serve hot.

Nutrition Information Per Serving:
- Total Fat: 1 gram
- Carbohydrates: 4 grams
- Protein: 1 gram

Bacon Egg Salad

Servings: 8-10
Time Required: About 25 minutes

Ingredients:
- 10 eggs
- 5 slices bacon
- 2 Tbsp. mayonnaise
- 1 tsp. Dijon mustard
- ¼ tsp. smoked paprika
- 1 spring onion, diced
- Salt and pepper to taste

Directions:
1. Place the eggs in a large pot covered with an inch of cold water. Bring the water to a boil and boil the eggs for 8-10 minutes. Remove them and cool them quickly in cold water.
2. Shell the eggs and transfer them to a cutting board. Chop the eggs coarsely and transfer to a mixing bowl.
3. In a large skillet, sauté the bacon until it's crispy, then carefully add the bacon and its fat to the chopped eggs.
4. Add the rest of the ingredients to the mixing bowl toss well to combine.
5. Serve garnished with chopped chives.

Nutrition Information Per Serving:
- Total Fat: 26 grams
- Carbohydrates: 2 grams
- Protein: 16 grams

Creamy Cauliflower with Cheese

Servings: 4
Time Required: About 45 minutes

Ingredients:
- 2 cups cauliflower, riced
- 2 Tbsp. cream cheese
- ½ cup half and half
- ½ cup cheddar cheese, grated
- Salt and Pepper to taste

Directions:
1. Preheat oven to 400 degrees Fahrenheit.
2. Combine all the ingredients in a baking dish. Cover the dish with aluminum foil.
3. Place the baking dish on the oven's center rack and roast until cauliflower is tender and cheese is bubbly and beginning to brown, about 35 minutes.
4. Remove the baking dish and serve the cooked cauliflower hot.

Nutrition Information Per Serving:
- Total Fat: 10 grams
- Carbohydrates: 4 grams
- Protein: 5 grams

Garlic Spaghetti Squash

Servings: 1
Time Required: about 1 hour

Ingredients:
- 1 medium spaghetti squash
- 1 cup water
- 4 cloves garlic, minced
- 1 Tbsp. olive oil
- 1 tsp. salt
- 1/8 tsp. nutmeg

Directions:
1. With a sharp knife, carefully cut the squash in half crosswise, across the short length of the squash instead of along the longer axis.
2. Use a metal spoon to scoop the seeds and loose flesh out of the center of both halves of the squash.
3. Place the squash halves on a baking sheet, cut side down.
4. Place the baking sheet on the oven's center rack and roast until the squash is tender, about 45-50 minutes.
5. Remove the squash and, while it's still hot, carefully shred the flesh into spaghetti-like strands with a fork.
6. Heat the oil over medium-high heat in a large skillet. When the oil is hot, add the garlic and sauté just until fragrant, about 30 seconds.
7. Toss the garlic, salt and nutmeg with the shredded squash and serve hot. For an extra kick of flavor, sprinkle with freshly grated Parmesan cheese.

Nutrition Information Per Serving:
- Total Fat: 4 grams
- Carbohydrates: 13 grams
- Protein: 2 grams

Conclusion

Now you're armed with the science behind the ketogenic diet and a plethora of recipes so you can put the science to work for you. You've got the tools to transform a list of common, keto-friendly ingredients into irresistibly satisfying culinary creations. You've got everything you need to make the changes that will lead you to a healthier lifestyle. There's nothing standing in your way, and the path to a new you starts right here, right now.

Made in the USA
Columbia, SC
02 August 2018